GAME DAY

MEET THE
PEOPLE WHO
MAKE IT
HAPPEN

PASS

Kevin Sylvester

annick press
toronto + new york + vancouver

CONTENTS

INTRODUCTION

Every day, millions of people around the world show up or tune in to watch their favorite athletes compete in soccer, baseball, lacrosse, basketball, hockey – you name it. The athletes are the unquestionable stars, the visible face of the world of sports.

But behind each of these gifted men and women are dozens more people who work just as hard, are just as dedicated to their craft, and are just as much a part of the team. They are the people who mow the grass where the baseball players hit, run, and slide. They freeze the ice so that hockey players can skate, pass, and shoot. They enforce the rules to make sure the game is fair.

Medical staff and trainers are on the sidelines in case something goes wrong. These experts in pain and injuries can help heal a torn ligament, a twisted ankle, a bloodied lip – and sometimes a bruised ego.

There are people whose job is to serve the fans who pay good money to be at the big game. They are the ones who prepare the hot dogs and nacho chips, while others clean up the wrappers after the last out or the final buzzer.

Just like the athletes they support, these amazing people make sacrifices, giving up vacations, time with family and loved ones, sleep. You'll meet some of them in these pages, but there are many more out there. This book just touches the surface of this hidden world.

Maybe someday you'll become a professional athlete. Or maybe you'll be a team doctor, a broadcaster, a referee, or the person who yells, "Peanuts! Cold pop!" while walking up and down the aisles of the stadium. No matter which, you'll be an integral part of the experience of game day.

Chapter 1

GREEN THUMB

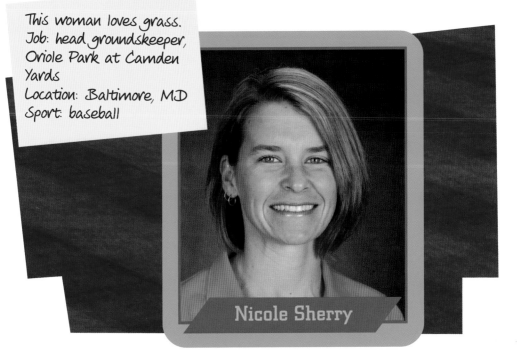

This woman loves grass.
Job: head groundskeeper,
Oriole Park at Camden
Yards
Location: Baltimore, MD
Sport: baseball

Nicole Sherry

Baltimore, top of the first inning: Miguel Tejada, third baseman for the Baltimore Orioles, makes a diving stab at a line drive. He strains every muscle to its limit, reaches impossibly far, and catches the ball in the very tip of his mitt. What an out!

Tejada stands up with a huge smile and waves to the cheering crowd.

Watching from a window in a special room in the right-field corner is Nicole Sherry. She narrows her eyes, takes a close look at Tejada, and frowns. She sees something the other fans don't – Tejada's jersey is covered with reddish-brown mud. "There's too much water on the infield," she says under her breath. "I'll have to fix that tomorrow and hope it doesn't rain."

Nicole Sherry is the head groundskeeper at one of baseball's shrines, Oriole Park at Camden Yards, home of the Baltimore Orioles. It's her job to make sure that the playing field is perfect for every game, no matter what the weather conditions.

We don't maintain just the grass but the dirt infield as well. We spray it with water every day to keep the dirt solid. That's better to run on and better to slide and play on. But rain can add extra moisture, and that's why you get muddy conditions. I hate that.

The dirt, a mixture of different clays, is pretty easy to maintain. Nicole and her crew rake it constantly to keep it loose and to remove any big chunks that have formed. If it rains a lot, they have a special powder they can put on the field to soak up the puddles – the same material, Nicole says, that you find in kitty litter.

But it's the grass that's the undisputed star of the ballpark's playing field. Natural grass is a huge part of the mystique of the game.

I don't like artificial grass. Baseball is meant to be played on the real thing. We use only Kentucky bluegrass because it's the best for the climate we live in and it looks great.

The baseball field stands out amid the concrete, steel, and brick of the bustling city. Its blanket of green suggests restful countryside, but weather conditions can make it hard for Nicole to keep it as green as it needs to be.

Baltimore is a weird city. It can be really cool one day and really warm the next. We get huge storms that dump loads of rain and then days in a row with no rain and boiling hot, humid weather. Going from one extreme to the other so quickly can literally shock

the grass. When I'm not on the field, I'm glued to the weather channel.

One of the secrets for dealing with rain is to plant the grass not on dirt, but on 100 percent sand.

That's why it drains so quickly. But there's a problem with that as well. It's a sterile environment. With no dirt, there are no nutrients in the soil for the grass to use as food, so we have to fertilize the grass every day. There's a lot of science involved. Too little and the grass starves. Too much and it will burn.

And there's an art to the job as well. Nicole isn't just the care-taker of a big lawn; she's taking care of the playing surface for a very finicky game. You can't have ridges in the surface or the ball might take a bad bounce at exactly the wrong time, such as when the Orioles are holding on to a slim lead. Grass is an ideal surface for players if they want to avoid injuries, but only if it's even and thick – and it's not easy to keep a giant field absolutely flat and plush. There's a lot to consider.

It needs to be cut every day so that it's always the right height. The ball needs to bounce well on the playing surface, so it can't be so long that it slows the ball down or so short that the ball skids on the surface. You also have to cut it twice, and you need to cut in different directions.

This is one of the stranger rules that Nicole has to follow, but it's something she's learned over time.

If you cut grass only one way, it will tend to grow only in that direction. That's because lawnmower blades cut at an angle, so

one side will always be longer than the other and it will grow unevenly. So cutting it one way and then the other makes it grow straight up.

Cutting grass twice in two different directions is the secret to making patterns on the grass. When you watch baseball games, you can see everything from rainbows to checkerboard patterns on the field. Besides looking pretty, the pattern helps trick the eye a bit by masking areas of unevenness or wear and tear. At Camden Yards, Nicole keeps the field patterns very simple, but the technique is the same:

We don't like to be showy, but when you mow one way it knocks the grass that way for a while. And we have rollers on the back of the mowers that rub the grass that way as well, to enhance the effect. Do one row one way and the next the other, and you end up with a pattern. It's like vacuuming a plush rug. When you go one way, it leaves a pattern in the fibers.

Nicole certainly knows her grass. And when she talks about it, you can hear awe in her voice.

I love grass. It's the most amazing plant in the world. You can cut it, dry it out, soak it, burn it even. It sleeps all winter and then gets punished every day of the spring and summer by forty guys who dive and run and slide all over it – and it comes back every time!

Her love of grass is based on an intimate knowledge of its wonderful blades and how best to grow and nurture them. That knowledge is the result of years of hard work. Nicole grew up in the city, in Delaware. She loved being outdoors but didn't see a lot of nature. Her parents weren't big gardeners either. But Nicole loved science, and one day her future appeared to her in the unlikely form of a peanut … sort of.

It was career day at my high school and someone from the agriculture department at the university brought along a box of Styrofoam peanuts, like you see in packing boxes. But these weren't actually Styrofoam – they were made from cornstarch.

I thought, How cool is that? *and I decided right then and there that I was going to study agronomy.*

At university Nicole took a course in lawn science and became fascinated by grass, and by the people who manipulate it to make golf courses and sports fields. She chose that as her major and spent the rest of her college career doing research on grass genetics, irrigation techniques, and landscaping.

Kentucky bluegrass is the king of grasses. It is durable and beautiful and can take a beating. It's used in almost every sport played on turf. But it's not blue – and it's not from Kentucky. The blades of grass are green. If it's allowed to go to seed, the flowers are blue, but that isn't allowed to happen on a sports field. And the grass isn't native to North America; colonists brought the seeds with them.

I don't have a green thumb in the traditional way, the way some people just love to see things grow. I have a passion for the science. I see sports fields like big labs, and we are always looking for ways to keep them in perfect shape, no matter what.

Nicole assumed she'd work at a golf course after graduation, simply because there are more jobs in that area for graduates from her program. She didn't realize it then, but fate was once more about to play a part in her life. One day the class went on a field trip – to see a real grass field. The trip was a tour of Camden Yards.

I thought it was an amazing place, and I started talking to the head groundskeeper at the time. He gave me his business card and I went back to school and finished my studies. Then, one day after graduating, I was watching an Orioles game on TV and I remembered the card. I was mulling over an offer from a golf course at the time, but decided I would call the Orioles first to see if they had any jobs.

They did. The groundskeeper remembered Nicole and had been impressed by her. She got an internship at Camden Yards, and there she learned firsthand how to make a great baseball field. Soon she was offered the head job at a field in Trenton, New Jersey. It was a minor-league team, but she would be in charge of everything.

I knew in my heart I would be back in Baltimore, but I learned a lot in Trenton. We didn't have as big a budget so we had to be more creative with fertilizer, water, and keeping the grass in great shape despite the punishment. It's just like being a baseball player. You need to spend some time in the minors honing your craft before you get the call-up.

Nicole honed her craft well: the field in Trenton was always considered one of the best. When the Orioles started looking for a head groundskeeper a few years later, she was ready. She applied for the job and has been there ever since.

There's a lot of pressure and a lot of sacrifice with this job. There are only thirty people like me in the major leagues and I'm in charge of one of the best stadiums. Summers are spent at the ballpark. I can't make it to barbecues at friends' houses or weddings or parties or dates. In some ways I measure my success by how much I've had to give up in order to be here, and I've given up a lot.

Back at the game, Nicole hears a clap of thunder in the distance. Miguel Tejada and the rest of the Orioles hear it as well and look up at the sky. Storm clouds are moving in quickly, and pretty soon the rain is going to fall like crazy. The head umpire glances over at Nicole. She nods back through the window and the umpires suspend the game. *Rain delay*: two of the worst words in the world for baseball players, fans, and groundskeepers.

It's time to get the tarp on the field. This is one of the biggest challenges of Nicole's job on game day.

Not every stadium uses natural grass. Artificial surfaces are used in many sports, from soccer to football. The Houston Astros installed one of the first turf fields in their new indoor stadium in the 1960s, and the name AstroTurf stuck as both a brand name and a generic name. Many players and fans didn't like the original versions, which were often harder and slicker than grass. Technological innovations have made the "turf" feel more like real grass, and it's a lot softer. When you see a player get tackled, you may notice a bunch of small dark bits flying into the air. These are rubber particles, often from old car tires, that have been added to the synthetic grass to make the surface bouncier and safer.

Let's put it this way: I'm in charge of twenty-six people, and only eight of them are full-time. The other eighteen are the tarp crew. They show up for each game, rain or shine, with one job and one job alone: to roll out the tarp in case of rain.

The tarp weighs two tons and it covers the entire baseball infield. You've probably seen it, rolled up like a giant green tortilla beside the baseball diamond. And it can be dangerous – St. Louis Cardinals left fielder Vince Coleman once got his leg caught in the tarp and missed the entire post-season because of his injury.

The tarp crew members have to be fast and strong and careful. They can get it on the field in just minutes, and off the field just as fast once the rain stops. They all have to know their place in the line that pushes the tarp, and they have to get there as quickly as possible. There's a lot of choreography.

The rain starts to come down in buckets. Nicole runs out onto the soaking wet grass, and she and the tarp crew quickly cover the

infield. Then she heads back to her room and checks the weather forecast. The storm is supposed to be violent but brief. The tarp will keep the infield fairly dry, but the outfield is another story. Most of the water will drain through the sand, but there will still be patches and puddles. One long sliding catch could bring up a huge divot. Oh well, if there's any damage to the grass they'll repair it after the game.

Nicole takes another look at the sky. Right now there's nothing to do but wait, so she heads back to her place in right field and indulges in a little daydreaming. She imagines the perfect day for a baseball game …

The perfect day for my grass is around 85 degrees Fahrenheit and no rain, not even the chance of rain. And it stays like that from when I show up at the ballpark at 8 a.m. until I leave at 8 p.m.

Does that day ever show up? Nicole glances up at the sky again, where a touch of blue is barely visible on the horizon.

Never. But I keep hoping. Until then, I'll just take the weather as it comes.

Chapter 2

STRAIGHT TO THE TOP

Albizu's purple baseball cap changed his life.
Job: hat designer, New Era Cap Company, Inc.
Location: Buffalo, NY
Sport: all sports—and movies too!

Albizu Rondon

You probably don't know Albizu Rondon, but you know his work. Albizu clearly remembers the day he knew he had "arrived" as one of the most popular (if still mostly anonymous) sportswear designers in the world.

He was sitting on his couch watching music videos, a great way to relax after a long day at work. A hip-hop video came on, which was cool because Albizu likes hip-hop. What happened next was even cooler. The singer's face suddenly filled the TV screen as he launched into his rap. On his head was a funky baseball cap with a redesigned New York Yankees logo. Albizu leaped to his feet. He couldn't believe his eyes. It was a cap he had designed just a few months before!

I called my wife into the room and told her to take a look. I called my family and told them to turn on the video. I called all my friends. I called everyone! Even after the video was over I was e-mailing everybody to tell them they keep an eye out for it. I don't even remember the song anymore, just the fact that it was the first time I had seen one of my designs on TV!

It was a New York Yankees cap with a twist. Instead of the traditional navy blue, it was white with striped piping and undervisor. It became a big seller after that video came out, and it wasn't just Albizu and his friends buying the caps.

I started seeing my designs everywhere. I would flip through magazines and see people wearing the caps I designed. It still blows me away, but maybe not my family anymore. I was walking with my little brother in the mall a while ago and I saw someone wearing my cap. I pointed to it with a smile, and my brother just yawned.

Chances are, if you've ever seen a rap video or a non-traditional baseball cap, you've seen a cap designed by Albizu. He's one of the lead designers at New Era Cap Company Inc., which is based in his hometown of Buffalo, New York. Albizu takes everything from team logos to mascots and then morphs them into original designs. It's hip fashion that has spread way beyond the baseball diamond, and Albizu has been a big part of that.

New Era had been making basic caps in team colors for Major League Baseball teams for years. Its success was dictated by how well it could make the same caps over and over again. Then one day there was a fateful phone call from film director Spike Lee. He wanted New Era to make him a red New York Yankees cap with a white logo instead of the traditional navy and white cap. Chris Koch, president of New Era at the time, said, "Sure, why not?" Lee wore the cap to the World Series that year and once people saw him wearing it, orders for that exact cap came pouring in. It was the beginning of a whole new era for New Era.

The ideas for new designs can come from almost anywhere. They all start with the shape of the traditional baseball cap – that basic look hasn't changed since Babe Ruth was in diapers. But within those restrictions there is plenty of room for creativity.

If you're designing a cap with a team logo, then you can't really change that. But no one says the rest of the cap has to be boring.

Take one of the pictures Albizu has on his Facebook page. He's wearing a St. Louis Cardinals cap, sort of. It has the Cardinals logo, but the cap itself is black, not red, and features swirling lines of white, yellow, green, and black.

I was on a flight to Las Vegas with another designer and we had some time to kill. I had a blank white cap in my bag. I took it out and we started talking about how we could have some fun. Bright colors were big then, and we had some markers with us, so we just started coloring the hat, drawing lines, adding little accents. We liked the way it turned out, so when we got back home we turned it into a cap.

New Era has made specialized caps in the past. In 1969 the company provided hats for the team that picked up the Apollo 11 astronauts when they splashed down after their mission to the moon. All the later moon shot recovery teams received these caps as well.

That's the creative part of the process, but there's lots of sweat as well. The initial design is just a prototype, and it can be as crazy as the designer wants.

My office is crammed with probably a hundred really cool caps with crazy designs – probably too crazy to sell to a general audience, yet. So we tone down some of them and that's what you see on the shelves.

There's constant pressure to be popular. New Era is a business, of course, and wants to stay at the top of the game. It's been making baseball caps for major-league teams since the 1930s. Today the business is driven as much by baseball cap collectors. That's where Albizu and the rest of the design team set themselves apart. Collectors don't just want hats that fit, they want caps that are unique works of art – wearable art, but art.

Albizu's desk is a hub of creative activity. There are pages of designs scattered all over the place. Caps are stacked on top of books and magazines and filing cabinets and chairs. Clippings are tacked onto every available space on the walls. He admits it looks as if a tornado has hit his office. His computer is almost hidden under the debris, and it's always warm.

We search blogs like crazy all day long, and it starts the second we get to work. We have to be ahead of what's cool, anticipating the new trends and looks, what people are talking about now, but also designing what people will be talking about in the future.

There are also two big Transformers action figures, a few other toys, and piles of comic books.

Everything is an inspiration – toys I had as a kid, cartoons I watched, cereals we ate. Movie studios often commission us to do caps to coincide with their big movie launches. I'm the comic book guy at New Era, and recently I designed the caps for Iron Man 2 *and* Alice in Wonderland. *It was easy to pick the colors for* Iron Man: *red and gold like the character, but then I picked a leather fabric that looked like shiny metal. That made the cap special.*

The New Era shop is like a big electronic beehive. The designers

e-mail files to each other all day, drop by each other's desks, and hold meetings to figure out what stays and what goes from each design. Then, finally, the cap is all set to be built. It's more complicated than you might think. There are twenty-two patented steps that range from cutting the fabric to putting the button on the top of the cap. Lots of stitching goes on in between to hold it all together.

The fabric seems small, but it can be a huge decision. Sometimes we can only alter a team logo or color scheme slightly. But if I use a shiny fabric or a faux leather, it can be true to the team and still be a cool new hat.

New Era even sells travel bags just for baseball caps, for people who want to carry their caps around with them. Like when Jay-Z goes on tour, perhaps. And people can now buy caps in Canada, Europe, South America, China, Japan, Australia … everywhere.

Why all this work to make a humble baseball cap? Albizu thinks he knows at least part of the reason.

It's synonymous with America. Every kid has jeans, sneakers, a T-shirt, and at least one baseball cap. It's what we grow up with and it's how we tell the world about ourselves. They are also a relatively cheap way to wear some cool fashion. Everybody wants to look different and a cap can help you do that.

Albizu says that for him, it goes back to when he was a kid growing up in a not-so-great part of Buffalo. He didn't have a lot of money for fancy clothes or fashion.

I was eight. My dad gave me a cap as a present. It was purple and black, and on the top, in white letters, he had a friend embroider my name. I wore that cap for, like, five years. I guess that was my first taste of a personalized cap. I didn't have a lot of money, no one had purple, and I never met another Albizu, so that was my big fashion statement.

Albizu sometimes marvels that he's been able to make it to the top of his profession, in a job that he is good at and that he loves.

I know guys who I grew up with who are in rougher places now than me. I had a lot of support from my family when I was a kid. My mom and dad instilled a sense of responsibility in me. I always tried hard in school and did well. In school, they nicknamed me Mr. Safety, but I'm obviously cool with that.

He had one other thing going for him: a talent for drawing. Albizu won a drawing contest in first grade, which began a lifelong relationship with pencil and paper. On the long subway ride to school, he would keep himself occupied and out of trouble by losing himself in his imagination.

Drawing is peace itself. I just loved the fact that I'd get on the subway with a piece of blank paper, and by the time I got to school it was filled with something completely new, that didn't exist except in my head.

Sometimes, he'd leave the sketches on the seat after he got up to leave. Maybe someone would pick them up and be inspired; maybe they'd try making art themselves. Maybe it would lead them on a better path.

Albizu did well in high school, and soon it was time for college. He decided to stay close to home, and he knew what he wanted to study. Surprisingly, given his career, it wasn't design.

I studied medical illustration for three years. In my view it's the highest level of illustration because it demands an intimate knowledge of so many details. You need to be accurate and creative at the same time. I learned how to be disciplined.

He helped pay for school by drawing caricatures at a nearby

amusement park. That work caught the eye of people who wanted personal portraits. He started making some money, but not enough to live on full-time. Art supplies aren't cheap, either. So Albizu knew he'd have to find a job outside the art world.

His job? He was hired as a doorman for the Hyatt Hotel in downtown Buffalo. But he still found a way to keep his artwork in the public eye.

What I would do is draw during my breaks and then I'd leave the sketches where people could see them. A number of guests and co-workers liked them and would hire me to draw their kids or their friends. I was able to keep my skills sharp even though I wasn't in the business.

Then one day his girlfriend – his future wife – told him he should follow his dreams and actually look for a job in design. By and large, Buffalo is not home to a booming economy, so he wasn't sure where to apply. But he flicked on his computer and started searching. Craigslist came up with an odd posting: someone was looking for a designer with expertise in a specific computer design program that Albizu had taught himself after college. And the job was in Buffalo – at New Era.

As Albizu admits, it was a really low-level job, but it was a foot in the door. He spent most of his time manipulating other people's designs, but he had learned an important lesson from his days on the subway and at the hotel: always make sure people know what you can do. He did his computer work, but he also drew during every available moment.

I left the pictures on my desk, making sure that anyone who walked by could see them. Within a few months the boss had

Designing an iconic logo is another challenge in sports. How do you sum up a game as complex as baseball with one image? Jerry Dior was faced with that challenge in the 1960s when he was asked to help celebrate the hundredth anniversary of the game. He says it came to him in a flash – a red, white, and blue silhouette of an anonymous batter preparing to swing. Dior says it's the one logo he's designed that hasn't been changed or updated. Today it's one of the most recognizable logos in sports, and it's stitched onto every official Major League Baseball cap and uniform. Dior was even honored with a special celebration on the field at Yankee Stadium for the fortieth anniversary of the logo.

asked to see my work. I was given a promotion to the design department, and just a few months after that I was made a designer.

It's been a meteoric rise. Albizu doesn't have to work as a doorman anymore. He is now established as one of the top designers in the business. He has designed caps that have been worn in baseball games, rap videos … and on the streets everywhere.

I was at a Kanye West concert once, in China. I was dancing and I looked over at the guy next to me. He was wearing my design! I just stopped cold. It was culture shock – like, wow! I felt like I wasn't just designing hats, I was helping out with international relations. If I ever have a bad day at work I just think about that and get right back to work.

Now all he has to do is figure out which pile of stuff his computer is under.

Chapter 3

THE AGENT

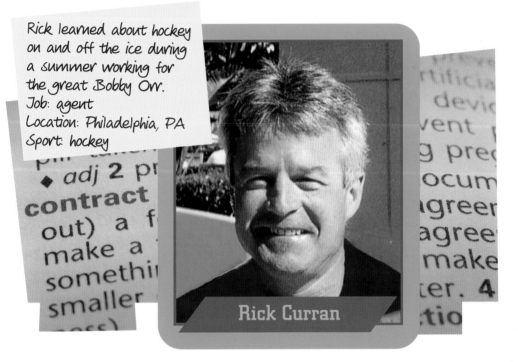

Rick learned about hockey on and off the ice during a summer working for the great Bobby Orr.
Job: agent
Location: Philadelphia, PA
Sport: hockey

Rick Curran

Rick Curran yawns and stretches, reaches a tired hand over to turn off his alarm clock. He rubs the sleep from his eyes. He can smell the coffee maker downstairs brewing a fresh cup. He puts on his sweatsuit and heads for the kitchen, catching a glimpse of his face in the hallway mirror. A little stubble. That's okay, he'll shave later. He heads through the hall to the kitchen to grab a bite to eat.

A few minutes later, armed with coffee, Rick arrives at work. He opens the door to his office, which was once a spare room over his garage. "Spare" is still the perfect way to describe the room. Aside from a huge TV screen that covers one wall, there are just two desks, two computers, and two phones. A handful of pictures hang on the walls, mostly of family.

You might not know it from the surroundings or the outfit he's wearing, but Rick is one of the most successful and powerful sports agents in the world of professional hockey. This room is where he runs his business.

I used to operate out of a downtown office, with big windows and a view of the city skyline. But it became totally unnecessary. More often than not I found myself meeting clients at their hotel or a restaurant when they came into town to play a game. Once the office became nothing more than an elaborate telephone booth, working out of my home became much more convenient and certainly more comfortable.

Rick sips his coffee. He was up late the night before, flipping back and forth between hockey games. Rick represents players from many different National Hockey League teams. He watches his clients to monitor their play, making notes on their level of performance and how much playing time they are getting.

It's more than just a professional relationship. Over time we often develop a close friendship with our clients. To us they are more than the superstar athlete as seen by others. As mentors we take pride in helping them adjust to the life of being a young professional hockey player.

Rick meets these players when they are quite young – kids who are blessed with skills and ability but are less equipped to deal with the challenges of living in an adult world as a highly paid athlete. An agent takes on many roles.

We are not their parents but often find ourselves providing them

Rick (right) with hockey great and business partner Bobby Orr.

with parental advice. More than once I've helped a young player deliberate by saying, "If you were my son, knowing what I know, here's what I suggest you do." The decisions are theirs to make; we just try to make sure they have a clear picture of what their options are. We try to provide them with continued support and guidance. We are also not their coaches, so we don't try to tell them how to play. However, we do remind them of their responsibility to the game and their teammates.

That's why Rick spends every night glued to his television screen as he cruises between games.

Glancing at his notes, he takes another sip of coffee, refreshing himself before his morning conference call. Rick hits the top button on the telephone's speed dial. There's a click, and then a familiar voice: "Good morning, Rick."

It's Bobby Orr on the other end of the phone. For people who don't know how significant that is, Bobby was arguably the greatest player to lace on skates in the history of the game, and Rick speaks

to him every morning. That's because Bobby Orr is Rick's partner in the player-agent business. They will spend the next hour reviewing their notes on the previous night's games.

We'll talk about our various clients and who might need a call. If their ice time is down, it may mean they're playing hurt or simply having a difficult time. If it appears serious enough, we might even put a call in to the respective team to see how they feel about how he's doing lately.

By the end of the call Rick will have a list of things to do and clients to phone. He may be heading into town later to meet a client for dinner. On a rare occasion, one of their clients may have committed a serious infraction, and Rick will have to respond to whatever disciplinary action the league might take. The solution may be as simple as a telephone conference call or as serious as heading to NHL headquarters in New York City for a hearing.

There's not a lot of idle chatter between Rick and Bobby when they get together on these daily calls. They are comfortable with each other, and they should be. They go way back.

Some of Rick's clients include Tomas Kaberle, Jeff Carter, Jason Spezza, and the Staal brothers: Eric, Jordan, and Marc.

I guess I was fifteen or sixteen when I was hired to work at the Bobby Orr–Mike Walton Sports Camp. I had known Bobby briefly since he'd spent a little time at the cottage next door to my grandparents. When they opened the camp, they offered my brother and me a job. We took it. It didn't pay very much that first summer, but it was a decision that changed my life.

Rick started as a junior counselor. Over the next ten years he did everything from tying up young campers' skates and assisting with on-ice drills to eventually working closely with the camp's director, Bill Watters. While others might have been mesmerized by Bobby and the other NHL stars at the camp, Rick focused on doing his job. He saw Bobby as his boss, not the demigod he'd become to most other people. And he learned some valuable lessons over those years.

Do your job and be professional about it. Don't be a floater or a hanger-on. Don't spend your day chasing the guys looking for autographs or trying to be part of their group. I learned to keep a respectable distance. Better to be seen working than heard talking about it. If I was asked to do something, I did it, and I tried to do it better than anyone else. When these same people who ran the camp went on to become important people in the world of hockey, they didn't forget about me, and I'll always be grateful for that.

One of those people was Bill Watters. Over the years Watters went from running the largest player-agent business in hockey to spending time in international hockey: world championships and Canada Cups. He eventually moved into management with the Toronto Maple Leafs of the NHL. As manager of Team Canada 1977, Watters gave the young Rick his first crack at the big time by hiring him as business manager of the team.

I brought the lessons I'd learned from the hockey camp. Dependability, for one. Bill had taken a chance on me and I wanted to make sure he'd never have a reason to regret that decision. Over the years I tried to be his "most valuable player." No one is ever really indispensable, but it's as close as you can come to ensuring that you'll always have your job.

Over the next three years Rick continued to assist Bill with international hockey. He quickly gained a reputation as a great organizer and businessperson. The timing was on his side for his next career move, but this story requires a quick history lesson about sports and business.

For years, especially in hockey, athletes had avoided forming unions. Most were happy to be paid *anything* to play the sport they loved, which was exploited by the people who owned the teams and ran the leagues. Players were paid far less than they were worth, receiving a very small portion of the big profits from professional sports. The team owners were making millions, but they shared only as much with the players as they wanted to – which wasn't much.

That started to change in the mid-1970s. Baseball was the first to challenge the old rules. Before then, the teams basically owned a player for life. Baseball's union challenged this custom, and a series of court decisions declared the practice unlawful. Sports leagues were ordered to give athletes the rights that employees in other fields enjoyed, including the right to change employers once their contracts had run out. This right has become known as free agency.

Suddenly athletes found that they could sell their services to the highest bidder, and teams were willing to pay a lot – millions of dollars rather than thousands. This led to a rash of great players, such as Reggie Jackson and Andy Messersmith, leaving their old teams for new ones that were willing to give them big contracts. Other sports saw this happening and wanted in on the action.

Free agency is common practice now, but it was a huge leap forward back then. By and large, athletes still weren't businesspeople, so they needed experts who could handle the negotiations and make sure the contracts were rock-solid. The era of the sports agent had begun, and through his association with the people he'd met at the Orr–Walton Sports Camp, Rick was at the forefront of the industry. Meanwhile, he continued to learn the business from Bill Watters.

The world of professional hockey is made up of a limited number of people. You learn quickly that your reputation precedes you.

I'm often asked if I have my law degree. Frankly, I never had time to get it. My continued education was less formal but probably more valuable to my career. I was very fortunate to get into this business when I did. I was introduced to every facet of the hockey business at every level of the game. I spent most of my nights watching junior hockey, listening and learning from numerous NHL scouts. Bill would take me to Maple Leaf Gardens, where I'd meet the general manager and coaches who were in to play the Leafs. Sure, I missed getting my law degree, but because of what I was doing I can put a call in to a general manager and know he'll take it. If I were a top graduate of Harvard law, I'd likely have to leave a message and hope it was returned in a day or two, by an assistant.

Rick's reputation for integrity ensures that a general manager will respect his opinion. As contentious as contract negotiations can be,

when there's a healthy respect for each other, it's usually just a matter of time before an agreement can be reached. Interestingly, when most people think about agents they usually talk about contracts and money – they think that's all an agent does. Rick laughs at that.

Negotiating contracts may be the focus of our work but, like the tip of an iceberg, it's only a small part of what we do every day. There's a massive amount of effort and preparation that goes on beneath the surface.

Rick estimates that as little as 20 percent of an agent's time is spent on the negotiation itself. It's hugely important and obviously has to be done right, but there's a particular period during which most of the contract work gets done. The critical date is July 1 – when a player whose contract term is up becomes a free agent. If he is classified as an unrestricted free agent, he will be free to sign with any other NHL team, with no compensation to his former team. Many general managers will already have been in contact with Rick, trying to sign their top players rather than risk losing them to another team that might be willing to pay them more money.

One of the reasons we keep such detailed notes is because it's not enough to simply tell a team how much money you want for one of your clients. You should be prepared to justify the amount you are asking for and be able to make your argument convincing enough that the team agrees with you that he is worth it.

Rick has worked as an agent for more than thirty years. In that time many changes have affected contract negotiations. More teams have been added, which means more job opportunities for players. But costs have risen: travel and equipment are more expensive. The

economy has had its good years and bad, and there's now a salary cap to contend with.

Rick brought his son Michael into the business three years ago. For the first two summers he sat at the other desk in the office above the garage. As a college business student, Michael became very good at helping prepare client files for contract negotiations. Now that he has graduated, he is currently enrolled in law school and continues to work in the office. His law background will help him become more familiar with the new collective bargaining agreement – the deal between the players' union and the league that governs all contracts.

> With millions of dollars at stake, there's bound to be some animosity. In 2004 there was even a labor war, which led to cancellation of the entire NHL season and a new collective bargaining agreement (contract) that put some limits on free agency. And in baseball, the World Series was cancelled in 1995 over stalled contract talks.

The new agreement is very different from the old one. Many of the rules that affect contract negotiations have changed. Old contracts aren't as relevant anymore. We basically boxed up many of the old files and put them away. The value of a player may be different, but the principle of good business has not changed. The people we deal with are still the same.

Most of the deals are completed quickly, but it takes a lot of work.

I don't get much sleep during that time. Either we're in the office working or I'm lying awake thinking about the deal we're working on. My wife brings in food and coffee and we work around the clock. Most of the deals are completed within a couple of weeks. The others need more time. Either we need to find a team willing to sign our client or the team may need more time to make room for him under their salary cap.

Of course, negotiations haven't always endeared agents to sports fans, who often feel betrayed when top players leave their teams or hold out for better contracts, sometimes skipping whole chunks of a season to back their demands. Rick says they are simply using the rights they have won through years of collective bargaining. No one is the good guy or the bad guy.

Our job is still to maximize our client's financial interests. But with the new agreement and the salary cap that each team must cope with, it's much more challenging to complete a deal that works for both the player and the team. As agents we are just one part of the hockey community. We all share a mutual interest in keeping our game healthy and successful.

Rick hadn't really kept in touch with Bobby Orr after those early years at the hockey camp. Orr had gone on to other things: playing, raising a family. But he later became a player agent himself, taking over a multi-sports agency based in Boston. This was an interesting step – Bobby had been burned by his own agent during his playing days, and he wanted to run a firm that was more responsive to the players' needs. A few years later, he and Rick ran into each other at an NHL draft. Shortly afterward, Bobby called him and they got together for lunch.

Although I was quite content with the group of clients I had, even I had to acknowledge that many of them were getting older and it was just a matter of time before retirement would deplete my company further. I hadn't recruited any new clients since 1992 and I knew I would have to make some decisions. Bobby and I ran into each other and one conversation led to another. I recognized his passion to be a positive influence on young hockey players. I'd like to

think he knew my reputation as an agent in the business. Along with a third partner, Paul Krepelka, we became the Orr Hockey Group.

Rick admits that he still had residual feelings of awe from his days at the camp, but it didn't take long for him to adjust to the fact that Bobby Orr was now his partner.

After they talk on the phone, Rick has set an agenda for the day ahead. One of his players isn't getting as much playing time as they had expected. Rick will give the team a call and see whether there's a problem.

When I call a general manager, I always keep in mind that it is his team and his responsibility to put together a winning combination of staff and players. I will not try to tell him how to do his job. The player, of course, just wants to play. If there's a problem we work toward a solution rather than wasting valuable time and energy on blame. There are times when the team might need to be a little more patient and understanding. There are times when the player is not doing what is expected, and certainly not what he is capable of. Those are moments when you have to trust your client–agent relationship. A client can't afford to have me tell him what he wants to hear as opposed to what he needs to hear. I need to be quite direct, making sure he understands where he needs to improve his game. He knows we'll be there to support him, but it is still up to him to get the job done.

Rick showers, shaves, and gets ready to tackle the other 80 percent of his business time, the personal side. With the players' schedules, this is most often done over the phone, but as often as possible Rick likes to meet face-to-face.

Months before the season began, Rick looked at the NHL schedule

and cross-referenced it with his list of clients. If the Carolina Hurricanes are coming into town for a game against the Flyers, he'll schedule dinner with Eric Staal and Cam Ward for the night before. If the Montreal Canadiens are coming in late following their game with the Rangers, then Rick will meet Tomas Plekanec for breakfast before the morning skate.

Although I'll be talking or texting with guys following games I've watched on television, there's no better opportunity to spend some quality time with a client than when they're on the road. Depending on the client and the time of the year, the conversation can range from "How are the kids doing?" to trade possibilities or pending contract matters.

It's another way that Rick's approach is a little different, more personal. Some agents try to do business outside the locker rooms, whereas he prefers to keep matters more private.

Going back to the lessons I learned from Bobby and Bill, the players' locker room is sacrosanct. We as agents do not belong in there. I don't even feel comfortable in the players' wives' room. If I'm at a game and know that a client would like to see me afterward to say hello, he knows I prefer to meet him off in a corridor or hallway, far from the locker or the wives' room area.

During the off-season, many of Rick's Philadelphia-area clients will drop by for dinner or to relax after a game of golf. Friends and neighbors are often surprised at how regular these guys are.

Hockey players have a well-deserved reputation for being among the nicest guys you would ever hope to meet and spend time with.

Many of them are almost embarrassed to be fussed over but are first to give an autograph or signed photo. They are just as comfortable standing around talking hockey with a group of fans as they are sitting around with some of their buddies from high school. They grew up much like we did. They know how much time and effort their parents sacrificed to make sure they could achieve their dream. They've been taught to know the value of a dollar and not to take what they have for granted. They know and appreciate how fortunate they are, and if they forget from time to time, we're there to remind them.

Rick doesn't see his clients as special just because they are professional athletes. He doesn't believe he's special just because he works with them every day. That may explain the shortage of pictures and memorabilia in his office, where only a couple items still hang on the wall. Wayne Gretzky's number-nine jersey that he wore with the Team Canada Juniors back in 1977 is framed. A painted rendition of the 1970 Stanley Cup–winning goal is signed by the goal scorer himself, Bobby Orr. It was a present he gave to Rick years ago, before they became business partners.

For Rick, the payoff of this life is twofold. Yes, he makes a good living representing professional athletes, but he seems to enjoy the relationships he has with his clients as much as anything else.

I've tried to make a difference in a client's career. I get a kick out of watching them succeed in life. A year ago one of my long-time clients was given a special night by his former NHL team. During his retirement speech he took a moment and publicly thanked me for my efforts and my friendship. For me, that said it all. I guess we both did something right.

Chapter 4

THE VOICE

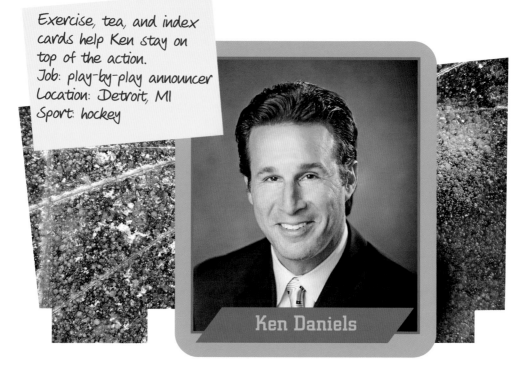

Exercise, tea, and index
cards help Ken stay on
top of the action.
Job: play-by-play announcer
Location: Detroit, MI
Sport: hockey

Ken Daniels

"Are you kidding me?!" Ken Daniels watches as his carefully organized
index cards spill all over the floor of the broadcast booth. The cards
fall under and all over the chair he's just bumped into – one of the
cleaning staff must have left it by the doorway. The cards lodge
themselves in between the microphones, headphones, and electrical
boxes that jostle for position in the booth. Luckily there's no breeze
inside the arena – it might blow the cards out the big opening that
overlooks the hockey rink, and then he'd never get them back.

The booth Ken is standing in is high above the ice surface at
Detroit's Joe Louis Arena, which is Ken's home away from home for
the NHL season. He is the play-by-play announcer for the mighty
Red Wings. Down below, the Wings and the visiting Los Angeles

Kings are just starting their warm-up, passing and shooting on the goalies. The opening faceoff is still a while away.

As Ken gathers up his cards, he sneaks a peek at the ice. Each player way down there corresponds to one of the cards he is putting back in their box.

I spend the off-season going over every player's career. I make up a card for each one. That's about seven hundred cards in all. I do them on the computer, one by one, and then print them off. It may sound crazy, but it helps me remember the information. Each card has its statistics, but also interesting stories about the player.

The information on the cards forms the backbone of how Ken will call the game. He doesn't just describe what's happing on the ice during the game. That's only part of his job.

Each game has its own storyline, which is not something people think about too much. A good game can tell its own story, of course, but not every game is a good one. And, of course, all games have down moments or breaks where nothing is happening on the ice. So I know if there's something compelling about a player or team that the audience should know.

Many of the stories are told in tandem with his partner in the broadcast booth, former NHL star Mickey Redmond. They have worked closely together since Ken joined the team, and they often finish each other's sentences.

It's like being on a hockey line together. We have a good routine. He can tell by my cadence when I'm inviting him to comment on the action. Sometimes we make eye contact and we can tell that the other

person has something to say. And we have a lot of fun. That comes across – the audience can feel like they are in the booth with us.

Ken (right) and broadcast partner Mickey Redmond.

Team sports are rich with stories, and Ken and Mickey weave them into the broadcast. They discuss rookies who are trying to break into the NHL, players who are dealing with injuries, and teams that are fighting for a playoff spot.

It sounds off the cuff, but that's part of good performance skills. The informality is really the result of good preparation. If you're not prepared, you stumble and hem and haw as you search your brain for information. It's not good to listen to.

All the stories are in those freshly arranged cards – and in Ken's brain. Not surprisingly, he collected hockey cards as a kid. He grew up in Toronto, Ontario, where hockey was a big part of his child-hood. Ken played, but he really got a kick out of watching and describing the action, and not just for the hometown Maple Leafs.

I remember that I had a yellow plastic Panasonic radio, and it was a like a magic box. It could pick up the signal from one of the first great sports stations – KMOX in St. Louis. I used to tune it in carefully and then I'd fall asleep listening to the sound of Dan Kelly calling play-by-play of games hundreds of miles away.

Ken was always the kid doing play-by-play of his own goals in street hockey or his hits in baseball. Pretty soon he was describing all the action he could. He would even type up sportscasts on his typewriter and then read them in front of the mirror.

I had a passion for it. I wanted to be on TV and I was determined to get there. So when I was about fifteen, I started sending out letters and making phone calls to all my favorite sportscasters. One day Brian Williams, one of the best, actually called me back! I had called him over and over and over. He let me visit and watch him at work, and that just made me more determined than ever.

Ken learned a lot about broadcasting from Williams and others. He learned that you need to be prepared and knowledgeable about whatever sport you're calling.

What happens when a panel of glass breaks during a game? It can take ten minutes to fix that, and you'd better have something interesting to say or the viewers are going to want to turn you off. You also have to be observant about the game. Is it a bit of a snooze-fest? Then don't pretend it's not. If it's a great game, don't get too excited because then you're getting in the way of the action.

Ken learned even more about hockey from the inside, as an on-ice official. He would work multiple nights a week to earn enough to

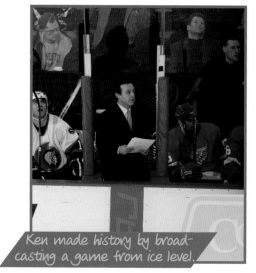

Ken made history by broadcasting a game from ice level.

pay for university. It gave him a respect for the people who call the game as well as for those playing. And he took any job he could in sports broadcasting – weekends, overnights, early mornings. He listened to the way Williams and others reported on sports and called games and then he practiced writing and broadcasting out loud to himself.

There's a way to call a game that is different from just talking. You can tell when something is important or dramatic by the sound of a good announcer's voice. Pitch is also important. If you sound too low and mellow, you give the impression that you're bored with what's happening in the game. If you start too high, where do you go if the game gets really exciting?

Ken eventually got a talk show on the local cable-access channel. He covered minor hockey, which is a big deal in Toronto. He had to do the research and writing on his own. It was a great education. Soon he was ready to approach the people in charge of the networks.

Brian Williams had moved on in his career, leaving his job as sportscaster on the evening newscast. Ken was invited for a two-week audition – on air on weekends – and was hired. Soon he was doing the evening sports, almost exactly ten years after Williams had returned Ken's call and invited him for a visit.

I always respond to kids who write me because I know how much that meant to me when Brian took me seriously. And what an amazing job it was, taking over from him. I was living my dream. All that persistence when I was a kid paid off.

Much of the job involved reporting on scores and stories from that day's games, but Ken got an even bigger break in 1988. He was asked to be part of the broadcast crew for the 1988 Summer Olympic Games.

It was my first time doing real play-by-play. This was for summer sports, and I wasn't very good, quite frankly, and still had a lot to learn about how to call a sporting event. I had watched and learned from the best and practiced, but you really need to learn on the job, by actually doing play-by-play. There's so much you have to keep track of.

It is complicated. Information is coming at you from everywhere. There are TV monitors in front of you showing close-ups and replays. Statisticians are dropping reams of paper in front of you with information on the game so far. Directors are talking in your ear about impending commercial breaks or upcoming images that you need to talk about. There's your partner in the booth – the color commentator – who also wants to talk about the game. There's the noise of the crowd. Oh yeah, and there's also a game going on down there on the ice!

And all the time there are thousands of people watching at home who are ready to point out slip-ups.

I am amazed at the pickiness of the audience. You'd better get every stat right and call every play exactly as it happens or the letters

will come in. And some people complain about the smallest things. I've done a lot of college-level games, and I found out that if I wore a tie that had the color of one team but not the other, I'd get letters saying that I was biased! At least they are involved and listening, and that keeps us on our toes.

It was a baptism by fire, but Ken loved it. The pressure just made it sweeter when he did well, and he did do well. He started getting more and more work and went to more Olympic Games. Then he was hired to be one of the hosts of the celebrated *Hockey Night in Canada*. That also gave him a chance to call some games.

That was a real thrill. I grew up watching games on Hockey Night with the great play-by-play announcer Foster Hewitt, so to host it was something special. It also got me noticed by all the teams in the NHL, and when Detroit started looking for a new play-by-play announcer, I sent them an audition tape. They liked it and they called me up.

The Detroit Red Wings are one of the proudest franchises in sports. Detroit is nicknamed "Hockeytown USA," so this was huge.

The Red Wings keep on winning and winning. I've hosted three Stanley Cup parades since I got here. People ask me how the team succeeds, and I tell them, "It's a family." The Ilitch family owns the

team, and they treat every employee like part of that family. We all travel together – players, coaches, and the other broadcasters. We all stay in the same hotel. Everyone here knows that you are part of a bigger community.

Ken joined the team just as more and more foreign players started making it into the NHL. Now a large number of his index cards contain handwritten phonetic pronunciations of player names such as Ovechkin and Datsyuk.

I sometimes feel like I could teach foreign languages. I have to know that Finnish players stress the first syllable of their last names, while North Americans tend to stress the middle. There's a player named Tomáš Kopecký. He's Slovak, and his name is pronounced "koh-pet-ski" – with that "ski" sound on the end. We had people write to tell me I was pronouncing it incorrectly, so I eventually had him come on and say it himself.

Ken just laughs. He says he asks each player in the league the correct pronunciation before the season begins. If it says "ski" on his index card, then that "ski" comes straight from the player's mouth.

Speaking of mouths, there's an unexpected side-effect of being the official voice of a successful sports team. Ken calls a lot of exciting games, and that can put a stress on his vocal cords, and more.

Laryngitis is an occupational hazard. I've never totally lost my voice during a game, but I have had sore throats that made me sound like Kermit the Frog. I always make sure I'm having nothing but tea during the game because it soothes my throat.

Ken's pre-game ritual is designed to keep him as healthy as possible. He works out each day to keep his body well and he eats nutritious meals. The NHL season corresponds very closely to flu season, so he gets a flu shot each year.

I need to stay in shape. You have no idea how exhausting it is to call a game. At the end of the game I'm so famished that I eat a huge meal. Of course, then I need to burn it off at the gym the next morning.

Ken has reassembled his cards. He double-checks his equipment and then takes a big breath. In about half an hour he and Mickey will have to do their pre-game "stand-up." Basically it's a hello to the audience that airs just a few minutes before the puck is dropped.

The last thing he does before then is get his face ready. He heads to the washroom and shaves, if needed, then puts on a bit of makeup, just to cut the glare on his cheeks and nose.

Ken Daniels has starred in movies and on TV as well. His Olympics experience landed him a role as "Olympic host" in the NBC Movie of the Week *On Thin Ice: The Tai Babilonia Story*. He also appeared in a film with Tony Danza, *The Philadelphia Phenomenon*, and was a play-by-play voice for the CBS/CTV television series *Due South*.

HD [high definition] is changing the world of broadcasting. The audience can see every wrinkle and pore. That's why I make sure I don't need a shave right before the game. I may have to start wearing more makeup as I get older, but I don't like it much.

Ken opens his makeup bag and applies some powder to his face. He smiles at the thought

that the radio guys don't have to go through this. Radio has its benefits for sure. And in an odd way, radio provided Ken with one of his most memorable moments in Detroit.

Ken is the official TV voice of the Red Wings, but when the third round of the NHL playoffs begins, the local TV hosts don't call the games. Play-by-play crews from the big networks such as CBC and NBC take over. Only the regular radio crews continue to call the games.

It was the last day of the Stanley Cup finals. Ken Kal is the radio voice of the Wings, but he suddenly had laryngitis. I got to step in for him. I called the game, and with just a few minutes it looked like the Wings were going to clinch the Cup. Ken was with me, watching, so with twenty-five seconds left I turned to Ken and insisted he close out what I felt would be a Wings Cup victory. The Pittsburgh Penguins almost tied it up, but the Wings prevailed, which made for an exciting final moment from Ken, with his voice on the verge of breaking.

Once the improvised makeup session is over, Ken walks down the hallway, takes his seat in front of the microphone, and looks at Mickey. "Let's have a good one," he says. They smile and turn toward the waiting camera.

The hot glare of lights hits them as the director counts down in their headsets: "Five, four, three, two, one – you're on."

> Hockey broadcasts start with what's called an "opening tease," a montage of shots that tell the story of the game. Before he goes on camera, the announcer talks over these images, which are assembled by the director.

Just before he starts talking, Ken pauses to take in the moment. *I absolutely love what I do*, he thinks. Then it's time …

"Hello again, everyone – Ken Daniels alongside Mickey Redmond. Welcome to another great night of Red Wings hockey."

Chapter 5

THE GREASE MONKEY

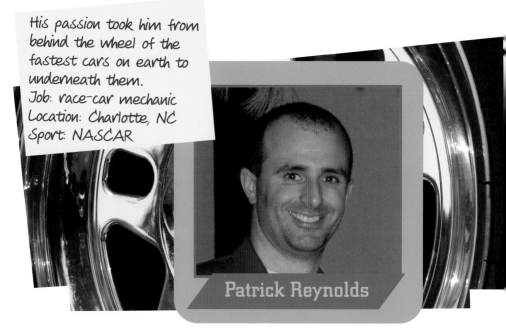

His passion took him from behind the wheel of the fastest cars on earth to underneath them.
Job: race-car mechanic
Location: Charlotte, NC
Sport: NASCAR

Patrick Reynolds

It's 6 a.m. Sunday morning – race day. Patrick Reynolds has already been up working for two hours. Right now he's adjusting the tire pressure on a hugely expensive NASCAR race car. You can probably guess that he's being *extremely* careful.

There's so much science, computer simulation, and aerodynamics that go into building a modern race car … and so much money. I have to control the tension and the excitement I feel on race day and concentrate like crazy on this amazing and expensive piece of machinery. This is no time for letting your nerves get the better of you.

It's painstaking work, and it can be messy, despite the precision that's required to fine-tune the car. Patrick often lies on his back under the car, moving around on a wheeled sled so he can see as much of its underbelly as possible. His team is just a few points away from some big prize money, if they can win today's race and move up in the overall standings.

As he slides under the engine block, Patrick catches a whiff of motor oil. For some people it's a dirty, disgusting smell. For Patrick, it's a smell that always pulls him back to the moment he fell in love with this world. He had just turned seven years old. His father, a former driver and racing nut, had brought Patrick to his first race, at the track near his hometown in Connecticut.

I guess you could say it was in my blood. I was hooked right from the start. I loved the roar of the engines, the squeal of the tires, and the incredible speed. That day changed my life.

Before the race, Patrick's dad had a surprise for him. He took Patrick down to the track to meet the driver. The boy stared in awe at the smiling man in his slick bodysuit and shiny helmet. "Hello, Patrick," the man said, shaking his hand. "Do you enjoy racing?"

Patrick nodded his head, which was now filled with one controlling thought, one dream.

I knew right then and there, in my head and heart, that I wanted to be the next great stock-car driver.

This dream became his obsession, even in school. He was often scolded for not paying more attention in class, but he kept staring out the window at the passing cars, thinking about how they worked, how they moved, how he could make them drive faster.

It was all I could think about. I got my dad to show me how a car worked. When I was old enough, I got behind the wheel and my

dad showed me how to drive. But to start a racing team, to be a driver, you need your own car.

Patrick spent his free time taking every odd job he could get, scrounging coins and small bills to buy his own car. It took him years of scrimping and saving and hard work to finally get enough.

It wasn't a great car. I learned a lot working on it to make it run. I learned firsthand that a stock car is completely different from the cars you see on the street. They are simpler, more pure – basically they are just a frame and an engine. There's science in the design, but the driver decides how much to press the gas pedal and how to get the most out of the engine.

For a while Patrick was able to live his dream. He competed in races and did well, but he also learned a big lesson about the business side of the racing world.

It doesn't matter how good you are. It takes a lot of money to get into racing, and even more money to stay in racing. You have to keep the car in top shape. There's gas, there's getting to and from races, parts, salaries, and on and on. My family wasn't wealthy, and I certainly wasn't wealthy.

Patrick tried to come back as a driver when he was twenty-eight, but, as he says, "a simple matter of finances put an end to that as well."

After far too short a time behind the wheel, Patrick's money ran out. His dream of being a driver was over at the age of twenty-two.

It was a tough blow, but Patrick didn't give up. He still had the racing bug and his passion for the sport. If he couldn't be a driver anymore, he'd use his experience to get another job in the business – but he'd have to leave home.

Patrick was able to drive his own car until he ran out of money.

I knew I still wanted to be part of NASCAR, and I knew there was only one place to go: the center of NASCAR racing, Dream City – Charlotte, North Carolina.

Patrick gathered up his favorite tools, hugged his rather shocked parents, and headed south. He had learned a lot about how to make a car run in tip-top shape. He didn't have a job, but he did have more than ten years of experience. Maybe he could become a mechanic.

I knocked on every garage door, résumé in hand. It helped that I had been a driver, and they could tell that I knew what I was talking about, but there was a lot of competition. This was the big time.

That's for sure. In NASCAR racing, millions of dollars are at stake in prize money and sponsorships. Every little advantage counts, and when the race starts, the car has to be in perfect shape. Patrick relied on his understanding of the driving world from the inside, as both a former driver and a man who knows how a car is put together. That finally got him through the garage door. And as soon as Patrick got work, his skills as a mechanic became apparent.

Patrick (right) and NASCAR legend Richard Petty.

I finally ended up with a part-time gig in a garage. I remember calling home to tell my mom and dad that I had found a job. They were worried when I left home, but they were so proud that I was following my dream. Drivers appreciate a good mechanic. They see my bruised knuckles and they know that I have paid my dues. They also know that this is a team sport, and everyone is important, everyone has a role to play.

He's had steady work ever since, not always with the same team, but always in NASCAR, always at the top tier of the sport.

Patrick is not alone in the garage on this race day, or on any race day. There are other mechanics on his team, and the crew chief is watching over everyone to make sure they get the car ready on time. Patrick has a checklist that is pages long. He needs to make sure each bolt is tight, each shock absorber is adjusted, each tire has the right pressure.

The one day you slack off and don't double-check – no, triple-check – everything is the day a bolt comes loose and the car crashes. No one wants that to happen and have it be their fault. You can't imagine the heartbreak when there's a crash.

It's not just the safety of the driver or the cost of the car that concerns the team. It's also the amount of time everyone has spent getting the car ready for the race, only to see all that work evaporate in a split second. After all, Patrick wants his driver to be safe and to *win*.

It's like being a kid again and you're on your way to school with that special art project you've slaved over, and then the wind comes up, grabs it, and drops it on the parking lot. It sucks.

Sometimes there's nothing you can do to prevent a crash. Auto racing is a risky, dangerous sport, with the cars traveling at more than 322 kilometers (200 miles) per hour. Races can be decided by 1/1000th of a second, so the drivers go all out to gain and then hold on to the lead.

It's not a chess tournament. We know stuff can go wrong. The trick is to be ready for the good and the bad.

Today's race is a big one. It's near the end of the season and his team is competing for money and points in the overall standings. Even the smallest change in the car's condition can make a huge difference once the race gets underway. It could also mean a big bonus if the team wins.

Mechanics do it for love of the sport more than the money. It's not a high-paying job, but it's a crucial one.

The mechanic's job is to make sure that the driver has the best machine possible under his butt, no matter what ends up happening during the race. Driver and crew are in constant contact during practice runs and races, getting a feel for the way the car is taking turns, running on straightaways, and cutting through the air as it thunders around the track. Patrick has already made adjustments based on the past few days of practice runs.

But accidents do happen.

The weirdest thing I've ever seen happened during a race. Our car caught fire, which isn't too weird in itself – people don't realize how hot those cars can get when they are running full bore. We put the fire out, but then the car kept catching fire over and over again. We couldn't figure it out. Then we went back to the garage and looked at the fluid we'd used to clean the exhaust shields of the car, one of the hottest parts during a race. There was a "flammable" sticker on the label. Oops.

Patrick shakes his head and makes a low whistle as he remembers that race. He checks to see that they are using the right cleaning fluid this time around. They are. Then he pulls out his wrench and triple-checks all the bolts on the car's frame … again. It seems ready.

Patrick wipes his dirty hands on a rag and takes another look at the clock. It's now 9 a.m. The race is still three hours away, which leaves time for yet one more run through his list. He slides his hand along the shiny metal of the door and peeks through the window at the driver's seat. He would desperately love to get behind the wheel, just to rev the motor once. But that isn't his life anymore.

Between now and race time the car will go through a strict series of inspections. To get it from test to test, it's Patrick's job to help push the car from station to station. Yes … *push* the car.

The fuel tank has to weigh the same as it will during race time. You run the engine for a bit during the morning to make sure it's working, but then you fill the tank and leave it alone. You want to keep miles and time off the engine until the race. So to move it around you use the good old-fashioned approach – your own two hands. And you'd better be in good shape for that because it takes a lot out of you. Stock cars are heavy.

How heavy? The rules say that stock cars can weigh no *less* than 1542 kilograms (3400 pounds). That's one of the things the inspectors will look at when they start their tests. They'll also check the car's weight balance. One side of Patrick's car will weigh more than the other, but that's legal.

Stock cars need to bank into steep turns on the track. To let the driver do that as fast as possible the left side carries slightly more weight. But if it carries too much weight, the officials will penalize the team. NASCAR has weight rules to keep us from building a crazy offset car that could tip over. Our weight adjustments are for speed and handling.

The shape of the car is also important. To make the race as even as possible, every NASCAR race car has the same shell. Inspectors use huge metal templates to make sure no one has altered the body of the car to get an aerodynamic advantage. The templates are lowered onto the cars and the officials take dozens of measurements to see how closely car and template match. Basically, if the car doesn't fit inside the template, it doesn't advance to the start line.

Then the officials examine the shock absorbers, the size of the fuel tank, the tire pressure, the brakes – test after test after test. It takes a while.

Patrick leans against the car to get it rolling. The lights of the garage shift across the shiny paint and sponsors' decals that cover every available surface of the car. It's amazing how much work has gone into the design. Patrick places his cheek against the cold metal and looks along the side of the car to make sure he hasn't overlooked any dents or dings. They would create a drag on the car when it's flying at top speed.

Patrick does wish he had paid a little more attention while he was daydreaming his way through school.

I had common sense and experience, but I really could have used a better understanding of geometry. So many of the newer crew members have degrees in engineering or computers, and that's how they are finding their way into the modern NASCAR world. It gets the doors opened for them ahead of guys like me. Of course, not many of them know what it's like to drive a stock car.

The inspection itself is like a laboratory experiment. Inspectors examine every detail. If they find something amiss, they can do anything from fining Patrick's team to actually confiscating the car. He shudders when he thinks how much work would go to waste if that happened.

The inspectors lower the huge aluminum template onto the car. Patrick can see that it fits perfectly. He smiles – the car is going to be cleared for the start line.

While he waits for the inspectors to finish, Patrick catches sight of the pit crew members getting their tools ready. During the race they will change the tires, fill the fuel tank, and make emergency adjustments to the car. This is another way in which the racing world has changed. Mechanics can be part of the pit crew – it's called "going over the wall," in reference to the low walls that separate the racetrack from the pit-stop area – but that is becoming rare.

Today the pit guys are often trained athletes with very specialized jobs. They are strong so they can lift tires easily, and some are runners because they can move really fast. They don't have to know how the whole car works, just how to get the tires on and off and how to fill the gas tank safely and quickly. They are very specialized.

Patrick tried his hand at driving a few years ago but again ran out of money.

The template is raised back up to the ceiling of the garage and the inspectors give Patrick's team the okay. Now they can push the car to the start area. In the hours that he's been here, this is the first time that Patrick has gotten close to the actual track. He can feel his feet tingle as they touch the sizzling asphalt.

He pushes the car into the pit area and allows himself a moment to take in his surroundings. The crowd has started to trickle in and a low, buzzing hum is beginning to travel around the oval stadium. It grows and grows as more people pass through the gates and find their seats. Once the race begins, the combination of rabid NASCAR fans and roaring engines will make the noise almost unbearable. It's electric.

Shortly the race will begin with the words "Gentlemen, start your engines." Patrick loves that moment. He takes a deep breath; an incredible sense of peace washes over him.

It's like I can see everything at that moment so clearly. The cars are gleaming. The people are smiling. It's everything I love about race day. The smells and sensations are so vivid. It's like that first day at the track when I was seven. Then the race starts, and it's back to work.

The green flag waves and the cars begin speeding around the track. Patrick stands on the pit road, on the garage side of the wall. He monitors the race closely, watching how the car is handling turns, how it's able to accelerate on the straightaways, and how well it's responding to the driver. His body moves and sways as he imagines himself behind the wheel.

The tools are all laid out in case there's a need for emergency repairs, but Patrick can tell things are going well; he and the team have done a good job. The car isn't just doing well, in fact – it's doing great, and with a few laps left, his driver surges into the lead. Patrick and the crew are mesmerized as they watch their car bank perfectly, then speed up to keep a safe distance between its rear bumper and the cars charging up from behind. The incredible force will test every bolt on the car, but Patrick isn't worried. This is where all that hard work and triple-checking pay off. Nothing is going to go wrong with this car today.

The driver roars into the final stretch and the checkered flag falls to signal the finish. Patrick and his team let out a loud whoop and dance around. They've won!

What a feeling! So much work has gone into the race. You can't describe it. But we don't have much time to celebrate.

All the top finishers have to go back for a second inspection. The car is weighed and measured again to make sure nothing was

altered during the race to give the team an unfair advantage. While that's happening, Patrick carefully packs up his tools. After a while the driver comes into the garage and thanks every member of the crew personally.

The fans don't always know how important the mechanic is, but the drivers all do. They couldn't race the car without a great team behind them.

Finally the car emerges. It's passed the secondary inspection. Now it has to be carefully cleaned and packed up in a metal container. It's then loaded onto the back of a truck and driven to the next race. Patrick packs his tools into the truck and then heads home.

One funny thing about getting home after the race is that, after you've helped a car go around a track at hundreds of miles per hour, you get stuck for an hour in all the post-race traffic. But at least the time passes more quickly when you've won.

Finally Patrick makes it home. He's too tired even to take a shower, so he just crashes on his bed. More than eighteen hours after his alarm clock woke him up in the dark, Patrick is finally able to rest. He lays his head on the pillow and is asleep within seconds. He dreams he's a seven-year-old boy again, standing next to his father at the racetrack. They are both smiling as the sound of revving engines fills their ears. Then a clear voice breaks in over the din: "Gentlemen, start your engines."

In his sleep, Patrick smiles.

Chapter 6

JUGGLING ACT

His calendar is always full.
Job: game scheduler
Location: Tampa, FL
Sport: lacrosse

Brian Lemon

The lives of athletes are often controlled by numbers, and the numbers change as the sport changes. How fast can a sprinter run? What's the top score the judges will give a gymnast for a great routine? What's the top batting average for a hitter in baseball?

But one set of numbers is crucial in every sport: the numbers on the yearly calendar – the schedule. Every sport has a schedule of big events, competitions, or games. When they are and where they are can hugely affect how well the athletes will perform and how successful the events will be.

Setting the schedule is a daunting task, and one of the hardest sports to schedule is professional lacrosse. It involves weeks of work – and lots of coffee. Brian Lemon, of the National Lacrosse League, knows how hard it can be.

Lacrosse is tough to schedule because we have teams all over North America, and we also play our season inside in the winter, in major arenas. Those arenas are also used by pro basketball and hockey teams. They have priority over us, quite frankly, so we have fewer open dates to work with.

That's just one concern Brian has to deal with. Lots of people want – and need – to have their say in the final list of dates. Brian starts the process months before the season begins. He looks at significant dates on the calendar for the upcoming year, which include everything from holidays to other big sporting and entertainment events. Then he sends a letter to the various teams in the league, asking them to avoid those dates.

Lacrosse was being played long before "professional sports" was even a thought in an organizer's head. Aboriginal peoples in North America played lacrosse games that would cover huge tracts of land. They called it "the Creator's game." European missionaries thought the curved sticks the Aboriginals used resembled a bishop's curved staff, or crosier – la crosse in French.

The National Lacrosse League has been around in one form or another since the 1980s. The game is played indoors, on a hockey rink covered with artificial turf.

For example, if I see that the Super Bowl is going to be on February 3, I tell teams they probably want to avoid that date because everyone will either be at or watching the Super Bowl. Each city also has big college games or local holidays that they may want to avoid or consider for a game.

Once that letter goes out to the teams, Brian waits for them to send back a list of the dates they really want. All teams want the best dates possible for their home games, of course, so if there's a free Saturday night in Orlando's arena – a coveted night in any sports league – the Orlando Titans will ask the league to make sure they can host a game that night. Of course, most of the other teams will look for that same date.

Once every team has sent in its wish list, Brian and the league crew get to work. This is where the large volumes of coffee come in.

Three or four teams may want to host a game on that same Saturday night. We want to keep everyone happy, or at least as happy as possible, so we sit in front of our computer and start plugging in possible dates. There are some givens, such as teams in the same division that have to meet – Buffalo and Toronto, for example – but there are lots of wild cards as well.

But wait – it's not just the teams that have an interest in the final schedule. Broadcasters also send along their wish lists for marquee matchups on prime nights. Maybe they want to see an Edmonton–Calgary game that night. That's good for the league too because it could mean a bigger TV audience. Brian has to cross-reference these requests with all the other requests.

We do have a bit of a tie-breaker when teams want the same thing: seniority. Teams that have been in the league longer get first dibs on big days such as January 2 – days with guaranteed big crowds. But that still leaves lots of figuring.

The process of scheduling takes days, and nights, of brain-racking effort. Why so long? Because of all the possible variations and interests … and potential pitfalls. Orlando may want to host a game one night, but the team might have to play in Colorado the next night. Sure, the team wants a prime date for a home game, but does it also want to exhaust its players by making them jump on a plane for a five-hour flight right afterward? It's a trade-off.

Brian knows all about the downside of badly assembled schedules. He was a player in the league for many years.

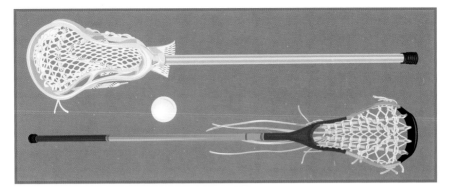

We always looked closely at the schedule as soon as it came out. Players don't like back-to-back games very much, for example. Lacrosse is a tough, physical sport. You really want at least a day off in between to rest your bruises before you step back into the arena.

On the flip side, a well-balanced schedule can actually help teams become more cohesive. For example, if there's a chunk of time built in to the schedule between a home game and a faraway road game, it can be a bonus.

Teams often like extra travel days because you hang together as a team and form bonds that help you play better. So we might book a longer road trip for a team from the East Coast that's heading to the West Coast. If every team gets something like that it makes for a more competitive league.

Brian tries to make sure the schedule is fair, but he also knows that underlying everything is the business. The National Lacrosse League is not made up of incredibly rich teams with private jets and stretch limousines.

It was something I learned when I became a league official. Business concerns are number one. Competition is number one-A. So every team needs as many games as possible that will attract fans. Buffalo and Toronto, for example, is a great draw, so we might add an extra game between those two teams in the season. And we can't avoid back-to-back games. Every team will end up with one or two a year.

Travel costs are a growing concern. Fuel price hikes and the rising cost of travel and accommodations have hit teams right in their already light pocketbooks. Lacrosse is not a wealthy sport like baseball or NFL football. Teams need to keep the travel to a minimum. This means the league is looking at more games between opponents whose cities are close together.

So, after considering all these concerns and (sometimes competing) interests, Brian finally emerges from his office with a finished schedule. Job done, right? Nope. Only if the stars are aligned in his favor.

Sometimes you set the schedule and then a rock band will announce a tour. They'll want a prime night and we get bumped.

*It doesn't happen often, but when it does we have to scramble a bit
to find another date. Tickets have to be reprinted. It can be a bit of
a mess.*

A mess, but a necessary one. At least there's no chance of a rain delay in an indoor arena. All this hard work means the players get the most balanced schedule possible, the fans get to go to home games on prime dates, and the broadcasters can show as many games as possible for the fans to see and hear at home.

Now Brian can relax and be more like a fan. He watches as many games as possible, ticking off the dates on the schedule he helped organize. The season will end, he hopes, with no problems or surprises.

Of course, even then the coffee machine and computer won't be shut off. One last job awaits the scheduler – the playoffs.

I have nightmares about that sometimes. If, say, Toronto makes the playoffs, that's fairly easy. But if the city's hockey and basketball teams are also in their playoffs? At the same time? Well, it can make your head spin.

A scheduling conflict is often a pain, but it can sometimes work out for the best. The Montreal Alouettes football team was scheduled to play a game in the cavernous domed Olympic Stadium. But the band U2 had booked the stadium for a concert. The Alouettes scrambled to find a new venue and they settled on the smaller, outdoor, and somewhat derelict stadium at McGill University. It even had tree roots growing out of parts of the concrete bleachers. But the fans fell in love with the quirky surroundings and outdoor charm. The Alouettes had trouble selling tickets at the "Big O," but they have sold out ever since moving to McGill. They've even had to build additional seating!

Chapter 7

ICE RUNS IN HIS VEINS

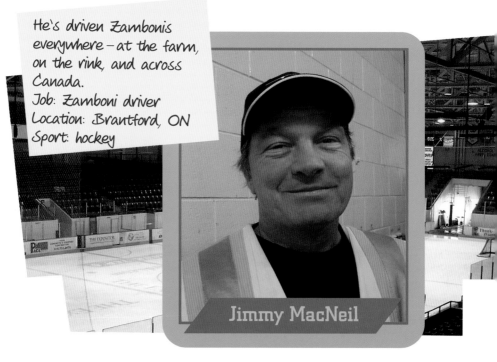

He's driven Zambonis everywhere – at the farm, on the rink, and across Canada.
Job: Zamboni driver
Location: Brantford, ON
Sport: hockey

Jimmy MacNeil

Jimmy MacNeil didn't just ride an ATV or a go-kart around the family farm when he was a kid. He also drove a Zamboni.

Dad would bring Zambonis back to the farm and we'd take them for rides up and down the road. It's in my blood. Our shop was full of them.

No wonder Jimmy grew up to be voted the greatest Zamboni driver in the world. It's true – it happened in 1999. He's even nicknamed "The Iceman."

But let's rewind a bit. Jimmy grew up on a farm outside Brantford, Ontario. His father, Alex, was well known as one of the best mechanics in the area. He was always helping out his neighbors with their tractors and harvesting machines, and he had a keen interest in Jeeps.

Then one night, back in the early 1960s, he got a call, really late. There was this new-fangled ice-resurfacing machine that had broken down and no one knew how to fix it. But it was built on a Jeep frame, so they wondered if my dad would have a look.

The machine was a Zamboni, the first of its kind in Canada. Jimmy's dad was able to fix it, and he did such a good job that he quickly became the go-to repair guy, and not just in Brantford.

He would get called all over the country to fix the machines, at all sorts of weird hours. They called him "Anytime Alex" because he was always willing to work on the Zambonis. He would take me along too. At first, when I was younger, I would bring my skates and go for a spin across the ice while he fixed the machine. Then when I got older, I used to help him out with the actual repairs. He became my teacher and one of my best friends. So my appreciation of how hard it is to make good ice goes way back.

Remarkably, the Zamboni wasn't invented in icy Canada but in one of the warmest parts of the United States. California's Frank Zamboni had worked as a mechanic and a designer of refrigerators. In 1940 he also partnered in a huge outdoor ice rink, and he tinkered with a way to resurface the ice more quickly than the old shovel-and-hose method. He matched his knowledge of cars with his knowledge of cooling units, and voila! – the Zamboni, which simultaneously scrapes and sweeps the ice and then lays down a thin film of warm water on top.

Other companies make ice-resurfacing machines as well, such as Olympia and the Icecat, a newcomer that runs on electricity.

In the long run, the MacNeils may have been too successful for their own good. Eventually the Zamboni company decided it was doing so well in Canada that it would open a new manufacturing plant

there. The company chose Brantford, and that was no coincidence.

We had become friends of the Zamboni family, so when they went looking for a place in Canada, they decided on our hometown. It was an honor, but it also signaled the end of my career as a repairman. Well, that and the fact that I had fallen in love.

Jimmy's dad repaired Zambonis on their family farm.

The two – love and business – were connected. Jimmy was about to get married when the Zambonis announced plans for their new plant. He would likely have a family to feed soon, so his father took him aside with some career advice. He told Jimmy that their business was going to shrink now that Zamboni had a Canadian foothold in his hometown. The company would soon open its own internal service department.

Jimmy was shocked. He looked at all the pictures of Zambonis his father had nailed up around his office. He felt a pang of sadness, but then Alex had a great idea. He knew that Jimmy loved working on Zambonis, so why not look for work that meant actually being on a Zamboni?

I looked for any job I could get working in a rink. I saw a notice that a small town – a really small town – was looking for a driver. I got the job. I spent a few years there and enjoyed it a lot. I learned more about how to make a perfect sheet of ice. Then there was an opening in my hometown and I grabbed that. It was at the Brantford Civic Centre. That's the same rink the Pittsburgh Penguins used for their training camp. I've been there ever since.

Lots of people think that the Zamboni driver does a few turns around the ice, then sits on his rear end for fifty minutes until it's time to resurface the ice again. That makes Jimmy laugh.

People have no idea how much the guy on the Zamboni does. For one thing, you don't just resurface the ice, which is an art; you are also in charge of the whole ice-making side of the rink operations. You keep the cooling unit running, the Zamboni running. Even with my experience I needed to go to school. You have to study to get certified as an ice technician. It's complicated work.

In Brantford the complicated work gets underway in August, weeks before the winter sports season begins. The ice from the previous season has melted away. First Jimmy and the crew at the Civic Centre have to check that the cooling system is working. The unit uses Freon gas to cool a salt-and-water mixture called brine. The salt keeps the brine from freezing as the temperature dips colder and colder. Pumps force the cooled brine through pipes buried in the concrete floor of the rink. Once the floor gets really cold, it's time to grab a huge hose and start flooding.

The trick is to flash-freeze the water in thin layers. So the concrete has to be really cold first. We start with laying down layer after

layer over a number of days. After building a good layer of ice we can take the Zamboni out to help build up the ice some more, until it's about a quarter-inch thick. Then the ice is painted white and the lines for the hockey rink are painted over that, and then we have to build the ice up by more flooding before it's ready to take skates.

Jimmy has to keep a close eye on the ancient cooling system.

The Civic Centre poses some challenges. The rink is so old that the concrete has buckled over time, making some spots higher than others. When you're flash-freezing water that can mean the ice will be uneven as well. The ice-makers have to be careful to make sure that the water is spread out so the top layer freezes as one smooth pad. It has to be at least half an inch thick as well, but not too thick, or else the bottom will be cold and the top warm. It's a tough balance that they have to get right. The rink will be punished over the next ten months by the toe-picks of figure skaters and the powerful slashing stops of hockey players, so the base needs to be solid.

It's hard work, and it's cold work.

I wear sweats, heavy jackets, and at least one pair of long johns underneath my clothes, and that's even before the really cold weather hits.

Once the season begins, it doesn't get any warmer and the work doesn't get any easier. The refrigeration unit has to be checked constantly. It keeps coolant running through the floor so that the ice stays hard and thick. One breakdown and the rink will start to melt.

The Zamboni needs to be monitored and maintained as well. It travels the equivalent of a cross-country trip each year. It has water tanks, pumps, and a huge, sharp blade that smoothes out the ice as it passes over it. It's an amazing machine that scrapes the ice surface, picks up the snow and throws it in a huge tank, then spreads a thin layer of hot water over the top of the rink.

Hot water binds better with the existing ice. It does all this while moving at a slow and steady clip around a slippery surface. We have studded tires too.

And this is where Jimmy really shines: the artistic side of making ice.

People know we have good ice at the rink, and it's a tough job to keep it that way. There are lots of things to keep in mind. You need to chisel along the boards by hand to make sure the ice doesn't build up there, where the Zamboni can't touch. Then, how much water do you put down? Too much and it won't freeze properly. Too little and it won't patch the gouged surface properly. If you don't time the turns right you can leave too much water in the middle, and that can affect the goaltender's crease. The athletes will tell you if the ice is good, and I feel proud when one of them says,

"Good ice tonight, Jimmy." They appreciate what we do because it makes their jobs better.

The biggest challenge after the wear and tear of skating is humidity. If the air inside the rink is too humid, the moisture can freeze on top of the ice as thin frost. This form of ice is too soft and flakes off, leaving dangerous ruts and chipped patches in the ice. It also makes it hard for the Zamboni to bond new layers of ice to the old. The worst-case scenario is a hot, humid day with a lot of hot, humid people packing the rink to watch a big game. That's often the case in the playoffs, when the games are the biggest.

Jimmy's motto is "Be prepared."

The Buffalo Sabres once hosted a game against Philadelphia that got so foggy the players had to take breaks. They skated around the ice trying to break up the mist. Buffalo won the game in overtime, but not until after one of the goaltenders had left the game because he couldn't see the puck.

If we know there's a big game and its warm outside, we cool the building down as much as we can. It's not just the weather that's a factor, but also the heat that a packed house full of fans will bring to the game. So that afternoon we turn out all the lights, which give off heat. We turn on all four of our dehumidifiers to get all the humidity out of the building. Then we watch the ice very carefully during the game, patching any ruts that appear, as soon as possible.

The crew will also stay at the rink for hours after the game patching any holes and taking extra passes around the rink to rebuild the top layer of ice.

Sometimes there will be a non-skating event at the rink, such as a concert or trade show. Jimmy and his crew lay huge sheets of plywood over the ice not only to keep it insulated but to create a floor.

Jimmy and his crew use plywood to cover and protect the ice during concerts and other events.

Other rinks use different insulated products, but we find the ice bounces back really well if we use plywood. It's old-fashioned, I suppose, but it works.

Jimmy loves his job. He says if he didn't, he'd be exhausted, and that's when you make mistakes.

Safety is key. You can do a lot of damage to someone if you forget to repair a rut or make sub-par ice. We host a top junior hockey team, and those players want to make it to the NHL someday, so they can't afford an injury. It's a lot of responsibility.

You get to know how ice behaves and how you can manipulate it to make your ice the best it can possibly be. Of course, this makes you an expert, but Jimmy says it also makes you a critic.

My son laughs when I take him to another rink to play hockey. I'll watch the guy resurface the ice and shake my head, saying, "Too much water; the puck will be slow," or "The ice is clear and dry;

fast game today, boys," and I pay as much attention to the action between the periods as I do to the game.

After scraping the ice, Jimmy dumps the snow outside.

This uncompromising approach to ice has made Jimmy one of the most celebrated Zamboni drivers in history. So how does a guy from a small rink in Brantford get named Zamboni Driver of the Year? It's a story about perseverance, hard work, and being in the right spot at the right time – a lot like driving a Zamboni, in fact.

The Zamboni company turned fifty back in 1999, and it decided to hold a contest to find the best Zamboni driver in the world. The announcement got a lot of attention, and soon people were nominating anyone famous who had ever been seen on a Zamboni. This included NHL-level drivers but also a number of famous movie stars who had driven Zambonis as promotional stunts at hockey games, such as Burt Reynolds and Matthew McConaughey. In Brantford this trend was not going over well with workers at the Zamboni plant.

They felt the driver should be an actual Zamboni driver, not a celebrity, so they all got together and put my name forward. Then

local radio and TV stations started calling on everyone to go to the website and vote for me. Pretty soon the campaign took on a life of its own.

A popular national TV talk-show host, Mike Bullard, heard about Jimmy and made him a *cause célèbre*. At the end of every show he called on viewers to support Jimmy. The votes started pouring in, and in no time Jimmy was challenging for the lead. His phone started ringing off the hook as reporters sensed a great story.

I felt like a celebrity. I guess I was a celebrity. I was being asked to do interviews all over Canada, then all over North America. I even got calls from national radio in England and France. Fans at the rink started giving me standing ovations and asking for autographs.

Jimmy had always been a local favorite, and he even had a regular gig on a rock radio station doing updates on music and sports, but this was getting crazy. Vote after vote poured in for the "little guy" who was up against the Hollywood stars and the big NHL Zamboni drivers. With just days to go, it became a race between Jimmy and Detroit's Al Sobotka. *Sports Illustrated* magazine ran a story on Jimmy, garnering even more support. Voting became so intense that it even crashed the website for a few days.

Finally the contest was over. Jimmy won easily, 177,560 votes to 97,265. He was gracious in accepting the award, thanking his family, the workers at the plant, and the city of Brantford. Above all he thanked his late father, Alex, who had been such a huge part of his life and who had died just before the contest was announced.

I can't express how much it meant to win that for my dad. I asked everyone to remember him. I also wanted people to know that this

victory didn't make me the best driver in the world, just a lucky one. It's funny, because I actually became friends with Al Sobotka and we've stayed in touch to this day.

Jimmy in his element, the Brantford Civic Centre.

Jimmy drove the Zamboni at the 1999 NHL All-Star game and was given a Zamboni-shaped trophy that he still treasures.

His fame hasn't ended with the contest, which so far has been the only one of its kind ever held. He still gets asked for autographs and still gets standing ovations. And he drove a Zamboni across Canada to raise awareness and money for grassroots hockey. It took him four months, and he enjoyed every minute of the trip.

Jimmy still lives on the family farm, although he says it's more of a hobby farm now. And he's glad his story has raised the profile of Zamboni drivers around the world.

People always talk about the athletes who earn a million dollars a year to skate around the ice. But if guys like me don't make the ice in the first place, they can't do a thing.

Chapter 8

TIMING IS EVERYTHING

Bob and his team keep
things running like clock-
work.
Job: timekeeper
Location: Memphis, TN
Sport: basketball

HOME

103

TO

BONUS

TIME

SCORE

PERIOD

Bob Young

Bob Young's job involves pushing buttons that say Start and Stop in the midst of the fastest game in the world, occasionally doing his best to avoid a 250-pound basketball player flying through the air right toward him.

You just hope you're quick enough to avoid him and the basket-balls that occasionally fly at your head.

Timing is everything when you are the official timekeeper for the NBA's Memphis Grizzlies. It's a deceptively simple and incredibly important part of the game. Basketball is controlled by time. Teams have twenty-four seconds to take a shot or they lose the ball. Games

Basketball players can be really big or really small. Shaquille O'Neal, for example, weighs in at around 147 kilograms (325 pounds). Of course, he's a center, and they tend to be big guys who can bang and bump under the basket. Guards tend to be smaller. Earl Boykins comes in at around 59 kilograms (130 pounds). Which one would you prefer to be flying at you as he goes after a loose ball? Luckily, Bob points out, this rarely happens. The bigger challenge is concentrating on the action with all the noise and movement going on around you.

are often decided in the final few fractions of a second. Every tick of the clock counts.

Bob calls himself the Guardian of the Game Clock, and that's not an idle boast.

If we don't know our job and don't do it well, it can seriously hurt the game, creating a lot of confusion. We might have to halt the game to correct mistakes and that can interrupt the flow of a game. Our role is as an extension of the on-court officials. The better we do our jobs, the better the game officials can do theirs. It's all about communication and supporting each other from the table to – and for – the officials on the floor. It's all about teamwork.

The "table" is just that – a table set up right next to the basketball court at mid-court. Bob sits there and keeps track of the overall time left in the game. Next to him are more officials. One is in charge of the twenty-four-second shot clock. Another keeps track of the score and the number of fouls each team has committed. These numbers are all posted and updated on the score clock in the arena and on the TV screens at home.

These are quite possibly the best seats in the house, incredibly close to the action (thus the need to avoid the occasional 250-pound flying guy). And they have to be great seats.

I need to see and hear everything that transpires on the court, and I mean everything. Did the ref blow the whistle? Then I have to

make sure the clock has stopped. In a split second we may need to coordinate with the production staff to be prepared to cue up a play for the official to review. We need to sound a specific horn at the correct time to signal a substitute and a different horn to signal time-outs and when play is to resume. We also have to ensure that the statistics of the game are captured correctly. Was that an assist, a team foul, or just a personal foul? All that affects how the game goes along, and as a team we have to get it right.

Bob has a computer terminal in front of him that has the Stop and Start buttons he uses to control the game clock. It also tells him whether he has stopped the clock or the on-court officials have. The computer has another button that sounds the horn to signal when time runs out or a stop in the action.

The officials carry precision timepieces on their belts that also stop and start the game clock, and if something malfunctions, Bob is the one who has to know what the real time should be. If the clock is inadvertently stopped and should be running, Bob makes sure it is restarted immediately. He notes how much time has elapsed and then, as soon as he can, informs the official. Then they make a decision about possibly adding more time to the clock.

In the last minute of the first three-quarters and the last two minutes of the fourth quarter, the officials concentrate on fouls and I'm

One famous last-second play changed the rules for timekeeping. Chicago and New York were tied near the end of a game in 1990. There was only a tenth of a second left. New York had the ball on the sidelines, and as soon as another player touched it the clock would start. New York threw the ball in and Trent Tucker caught it, turned, and shot, scoring a basket. New York had won. But Chicago argued that it was impossible to catch a basketball, turn, and shoot in that small amount of time. The NBA eventually agreed. While it didn't overturn the result of that game, it did rule that in the future any shot taken with three-tenths of a second or less left on the clock would be disallowed.

the only one who handles the time. It's intense because you need to avoid all the distractions, and there are many.

Distractions are plenty indeed. They include the noise of the crowd, flying basketballs, players yelling to each other, and coaches walking in front of the table to yell to their players or at the officials. The size of the players is a challenge as well – when a seven-foot-tall player stands in front of you, he blocks a lot of your field of vision. And there's no time for a bathroom break or a chance to grab a package of nachos from the snack bar.

You have to get into a zone, so to speak. I do that by spending the time before the game reviewing a list of all the things I need to keep track of during the game. It's time to leave personal things behind. For the next two and a half hours your thoughts and concentration are on doing the best job you possibly can, to ensure that the part of the game we are responsible for runs smoothly. And thus at the end of the game we have provided a service to the fans, to the players, the game officials, and ultimately to the game itself.

Mistakes do happen, but rarely. Sometimes you'll see the game stop for a few seconds while the time is double-checked. People often assume that it's a mechanical problem with the clock, but often one of the on-court officials has stopped or started the clock incorrectly. Bob has to know the right time so that the official can reset the clock to make sure the time is right.

The speed of the game and how quickly events take place is a great challenge, hence the importance of always staying focused. Things happen in splits of seconds, and those minute bits of time can have a profound effect on the game.

Bob and team sit courtside, with a clear view of the game.

The Grizzlies know how important the job is as well. When Bob was hired, he had to endure a three-hour interview and an on-court review of his first pre-season games.

They had to know that I knew the rules. I had been a referee for years before my knees gave out, so that was simple. But most of the interview was about me. They really wanted to know what kind of person I am. Not only do I need to be the type who can be organized and focused, but I have to be reliable. All the people at the table have to work together in stressful situations.

The table is definitely a team. They all wear identical Grizzlies polo shirts (the team gives them two each year before the season begins). They meet together before the game and eat together. They have to be a unit.

In the fast pace of a game you have to rely on each other. I'm handling

the game clock, so I'm watching the game to make sure the total time is right, but we are also backing each other up on everything else. We all have to know the rules so we know what kind of foul has been called or whether a shot was worth three points or two points. If one of us misses something because we were blocked out, we know someone else will have the info.

Technology is a huge part of getting the calls right. The stats crew members chart each play and can instantaneously review it to double-check what really happened.

There's also an art to timing the game and letting everyone know what's going on. Sometimes you can't hear anything, so you watch the officials' hands to know whether they've called a foul. Sometimes they are signaling to Bob that they need to see a TV replay for a close play. He knows to mark the time of the play so that the TV crew can find it easily and quickly.

And then there's the little-known art of sounding the horn.

If you push it hard you get a long blast. The players know this means there's a media time-out – a long break for them – and they relax. If there's a substitution, you want a short blast, so the players know they need to stay ready for the game to restart quickly. You don't want to get that mixed up because it can knock the players out of focus, and that could kill their momentum.

It's clear that Bob takes his job seriously. He knows from experience how important the details are. (He also knows how important time is – his full-time job is with FedEx!) The league has recognized his abilities many times and he's been a regular fixture in the post-season. In 2008 he was chosen to work games 3 and 4 of the NBA finals as the official clock operator. That was an emotional time for

him, both professionally and personally. His voice cracks as he remembers working the playoff games in his hometown, Los Angeles.

Bob and his mother. She was proud to see him work the NBA playoffs before she passed away.

I grew up in southern California and my mother was the biggest Lakers fan in the world. But my mom was perhaps the only person in southern California who would be seen around town proudly wearing a Grizzlies hat. When people would ask her about the hat, it was just an opportunity for her, with a smile, to share with others about her son who is the official clock operator for the Memphis Grizzlies.

Bob's mother was so proud of him that she also told everyone her son had made the NBA finals along with her team. She even sent Bob a note thanking him for sharing the moment with her. She died of lung cancer a year later, shortly after watching, from her hospital bed, her Lakers win the NBA championship.

That note and being in that final … it meant more to her and to me than you can possibly imagine. I still carry that card with me every day as a reminder of this wonderful game that she loved so much.

Chapter 9

CUTS AND BRUISES

A horrible accident opened his eyes to a different side of sports.
Job: chief physiotherapist
Location: Vancouver, BC
Sport: soccer, the Olympics

Marc Rizzardo

Marc Rizzardo rushes onto the brilliant green soccer pitch. He's dressed in shorts and a polo shirt and he's running as fast as he can. Only an incredibly observant person could detect the slight limp in his gait. One of his legs is a bit shorter than the other, the result of a work accident that curtailed his soccer career. In a roundabout way that injury led him here, to this hot, sticky summer day a world away from home.

"Here" is the soccer stadium at the 2008 Summer Olympic Games in Beijing. Marc is here as the chief physiotherapist for the Canadian women's soccer team, and he has a look of concern on his face. One of the team's top players, Brittany Timko, is writhing in pain. She's just collided violently with the goaltender of the US team.

Marc knows all about pain, which explains the roundabout way he's arrived at this scene. When he was sixteen, he was working in a woodshop. He was helping to carry some huge sheets of plywood when suddenly the weight of the wood was too much to control. Marc tried to escape, but a sheet caught his right leg, crushing it.

I almost died. It was such a severe injury that I spent four months in hospital. When I was allowed to go home, I had to wear a full chest-to-toe body cast. What fascinated me was the amount of work the physiotherapists put into helping me walk again. I was able to see the world of sports injuries from both sides.

Marc knew he would someday follow in the therapists' footsteps. Yes, it was a way to stay involved in sports, but it was also a way to help others who have suffered injuries. That's what Marc is doing now on the Olympic soccer field. Canada is relying on Brittany's stellar play to win a medal at these games. Marc's job is to see if she can still play or if her game, and possibly her tournament, is over. It doesn't take very long for someone with his expertise to make that call.

It was a horrible moment. I could tell right away she was seriously injured. It's hard to tell a player they have to leave the game, but there was no question. She had a look of panic in her eyes and was having trouble breathing. These athletes spend four years training to get here, and it's sad to see it end this way.

Marc immediately gets Brittany off the field and into the medical room in the stadium. It turns out that she has cracked ribs and a punctured lung. Marc is relieved that he was able to get her to the room quickly. The rest of the medical staff take over from there, running tests and making sure she's going to be okay. A full complement

Marc helps one of his clients work on strengthening her legs.

of trained medical staff with all the best equipment is on hand at such big events, and the athletes get top-notch care.

Marc is part of a team of health-care providers. The Canadian team at the Olympics has a larger-than-normal contingent that includes Marc, a massage therapist, a chiropractor, and the team physician. This large staff is a luxury, however, not the normal state of affairs. At many tournaments it's often up to Marc to handle all these jobs himself. He is a one-person on-site medical team, so he has to be an expert in everything from diagnosis to how to stitch up cuts, stabilize someone's neck, and much more.

You often handle everything from nutrition to psychotherapy. You work out a menu plan and order the food, then you do the pre-game warm-ups, the pre-game massages, and you also talk to the players to make sure they are in a positive frame of mind for the game.

Marc stays until he's confident that Brittany is in good hands, then he returns to the sidelines and hopes he won't have to deal with any more disasters. But he knows that elite sports are full of injuries, and that soccer is rougher than it appears to non–sports

fans. He's seen more than his share of concussions, fractured skulls, bloody noses, and broken bones.

Sure enough, later in the game Marc has to run out onto the field again. Goaltender Erin McLeod has torn a ligament in her knee. Marc knows her Olympic tournament is over as well.

She'd heard her knee go pop making a save. I told her to take thirty seconds to see if she could walk. I knew she couldn't, but sometimes it's important to let them make the final decision. They trust me to be honest with them.

That trust has been built up over years of dealing with the players. They will often tell Marc things they won't tell their coach. And he needs to know those things to help the athletes compete but also stay healthy for life after sports.

I have had a run-in with a coach. Coaches want to win and the players want to win, so sometimes the coaching staff will exploit that sentiment and ask a player to play through an injury. If I feel that is putting the player at risk, I'll say no, they can't play.

Today, with Brittany and Erin, that's not a battle Marc has to worry about. They are clearly too injured to play again in Beijing. Without two of its top players, Canada loses 2–1 in overtime. Marc leaves the field disappointed but satisfied that they got prompt and good medical attention.

They both thanked me, which is a sign that we have a good relationship, both professionally and as teammates of a sort. I know that some players wouldn't be playing at all anymore if it weren't for the work that the therapists perform.

Amazingly, Brittany Timko stays on with the team for a few days after the game to sightsee in Beijing. Her ribs and lung need only time to heal. Erin McLeod catches the first flight home to get ready for surgery and the rehabilitation that she is going to need to recover.

Marc decides to head back home as well. His job will continue after the Olympic tournament is over. He will help monitor Erin and a host of other athletes once he's back in Canada. Besides traveling with the team, he also runs a physiotherapy clinic in Vancouver that helps athletes to train and to deal with injuries.

Athletes are amazing people. They have something in them that helps them train harder, work through more pain than everyday people, even people who exercise a lot. They will punish themselves in the gym for four hours a day, while most people tire after an hour. I have a retired hockey player, Kirk MacLean, who comes to work out. He works harder than people half his age, and he's only getting ready for pickup hockey now.

Marc has also worked hard to get to the top of his profession. He has been a coach, a trainer, and part of the medical team for the Pan-Am Games, the Olympics, and dozens of other sporting events. He has also earned two degrees in human kinetics, a degree in rehabilitation medicine, and a diploma in sports physiotherapy. Even with all of that schooling he is always studying and keeping up with the latest technology and science.

Today it's way more complicated than just using weights, massage, stretches, and exercise. We have to know how to use lasers, stimulate muscles with electrodes, design exercise regimes, and monitor their nutrition if necessary, and so much more. The human body and mind are incredible, and deeply mysterious.

It's a year-round job. Marc's responsibilities also include helping athletes head off possible injuries. An ounce of prevention is worth a pound of cure, as the saying goes. He will work with the athletes to set up off-season training routines, an exhaustive list of workouts and fitness goals.

The overarching idea is to have the players peak during the season, so pacing is also key. You have the athletes start with small steps, then build up toward the beginning of the season, whether it's soccer in the summer or skiing in the winter.

Soccer players need to stay flexible, so they plan lots of stretching exercises for the winter months. They also set goals for weight training and runs so their stamina doesn't suffer when they aren't playing. Skiers do much the same but in reverse, spending the snowless summers riding bikes, jumping on trampolines, and lifting weights.

Marc sometimes finds himself wishing he too could play sports at this level again, but no amount of rehab is going to achieve that. At the next soccer game, probably on a weekend, he will take his place on the sidelines, between the coach and the players. He'll watch the game closely, always looking for any signs of pain or injury.

For the rest of the week Marc will be back in the clinic. Then there's all the work of keeping up with the latest advances in treatment and diagnosis. Anyone who thinks a life in medicine is easy is crazy. But Marc doesn't mind it a bit.

I see many people who don't work as hard as I have to but who are unhappy. I love what I do. I get to travel. I am around amazing athletes, amazing people. It's funny to think that an accident when I was sixteen helped me get to this place today. You just never know how life will turn out.

Chapter 10

THE EYES

He looks not only for exceptional talent, but also exceptional character.
Job: scout
Location: Chandler, AZ
Sport: baseball

John Kazanas

John Kazanas munches meditatively on his hot-dog bun with relish and mustard – he's not a huge fan of ballpark concession stands. John is the only one sitting in the stands, which is not surprising. Today's game is between two high school teams in Nevada, so most of the crowd will be parents and friends, and the first pitch is still an hour away.

John shields his eyes. The sun is blistering hot. The hot dog bun isn't. He shrugs and takes another bite. When you're a baseball scout, you take what you can get.

Scouts spend hours, days, weeks on the road. We go from park to park and state to state looking for the next great player. It can be an exhausting life, but I love it.

He must love it – he's been a scout for almost twenty years. At 185 centimeters (six feet, one inch) tall he has the athletic build of a former player. It's tough for him to sit still on the hard metal bleachers when he'd rather be down on the field taking part in the pre-game warm-ups. But his graying hair and his current job remind him that those days are long past. Still, John remembers growing up in Missouri and, after three failed attempts, the joy he felt at finally making his college team.

The coach told me that I wasn't the most talented player but that I showed a lot of effort and a lot of passion. It made it sweeter, in a way, than if I'd made the team right away. I also learned that talent is nothing without hard work.

John knows how tough it is to make it as a player. Today he has come to watch one player in particular, a young shortstop named Donny.* Most of the fans will watch how Donny does once the game has started. Did he get a hit? Did he get a strikeout? Did he play good defense? John is here early to watch everything else.

Every kid you scout has talent. But I watch how they talk to their teammates before the game, and how they talk to their coaches. Does he listen attentively and seriously? How hard is the kid warming up? Does he work hard in batting practice? Does he do some drills over and over to polish his mechanics? Sure, that stuff can be boring, but a dedicated baseball player, a player who wants to get better and better every day, will do those drills and try hard.

If he likes what he sees today, John is going to recommend that his team, the Chicago White Sox, pick up Donny in the upcoming minor-league draft.

---

*Donny is a composite of many great players whom John has watched.

John also looks for players who could develop into prospects down the road. He knows a lot of college coaches from his playing days and his days as a scout. If a player's skills fall a little short of the minor-league level, John might still suggest that player to a college coach. That means the player is good enough to make it to the next level of play but needs to develop.

So far John does like what he sees. Donny is taking ground ball after ground ball and making perfect throws to his teammates. He also gets along well with them, joking and smiling.

John makes notes in his latest journal.

I have hundreds of journals, going way back. I have notes on players who have made it to the major leagues, and plenty of others who haven't.

He marks down how fast Donny gets to each ground ball and how accurately he is able to read the speed of the hit. How quickly does he get the ball out of his glove and to the other players? John is also watching Donny's feet. Is he balanced? Does he throw the ball in a smooth and strong motion?

When John sees Donny bat, he'll record how well he hits the pitches and whether he swings greedily for a home run or is willing to make a sacrifice bunt to help his team. Does he stay away from certain pitches? Does he adjust his swing when he anticipates a different pitch? How fast does he get his hands through the hitting zone? The faster and more compact the swing, the better the hitter.

At the end, John will assemble his notes and rate Donny according to his own set of criteria. It's tough to score high in John's eyes. He once observed the young Albert Pujols, one of the best hitters in the history of the game, and marked him 75 out of 80.

The major-league average is 50. It's rare to find amateur players who have several average tools or better, let alone above-average tools.

Donny makes his way into the batting cage and gets ready to show off his offense. Ball after ball flies over the outfield wall. Anyone can hit home runs in batting practice, so John watches only the first two or three as they form graceful arcs in the sky. Then he turns his attention to the gathering crowd. He's looking for the kid's parents.

One of the most important things to look for while rating a player's defense is how deftly he is able to take a hard-hit ball into his glove, transfer it to his free hand, and then throw it on target. If this is done smoothly and effortlessly (or at least looks effortless), the player is said to have "soft hands." This is one of the biggest compliments a player can receive for defensive ability. If players seem to clutch the ball awkwardly and squeeze it hard, then they are more prone to errors.

It's one other piece of the puzzle. You can tell a lot by watching how they interact. Do the parents yell support or criticism? Do they yell at all? When Donny sees them in the stands, does he react with a smile, a nod, or not at all? Not all families are happy families. If the parents push too hard, the kid could end up cracking with all the pressure. He won't enjoy the game and can't relax. If they are too smothering, then the kid may not be grown-up enough to handle life away from home. If a player struggles with the mental part of the game, then that can bury him.

This is one area where scouts can differ in their opinion of a player – the intangibles, you could say. A few other scouts are now in the crowd, eating their own stale hot dogs and watching the same player. Maybe they won't see the same things John sees, the subtle clues about the kid's character or, as they say in the game, "makeup."

It can sometimes be 50 percent of what I'm looking at. A great player with a bad makeup isn't someone you want on your team. Baseball is a team sport, not an individual sport. Scouts from all

team sports, from basketball to football to hockey, they all have to
be aware of that. The team can decide a player is so talented that
it's worth the risk, but it's our job to make sure they know the
whole story.

Donny and his parents seem fine. He waves and smiles, and
they wave and smile back. The parents aren't sitting too close to the
dugout, where they could yell at him or the coaching staff. Distance
is a good thing. It suggests that Donny is growing up well rounded,
able to deal with the unpredictability of baseball – and of life.

The unpredictability of life hits people in unpredictable ways.
John sighs. He has four children of his own, two boys and two girls.
The boys have moved away, but the two teenage girls are at home
while he's out on the road. If he were home he'd be making dinner
for them right now. And it wouldn't be hot dogs; it might be a tasty
Greek dish such as souvlaki (John's last name is Kazanas, after all)
or some basic barbecue. He sighs again. He has learned a lot of new
recipes in the last while. He's had to; his wife, Christine, died of cancer
in 2003.

Christine was only forty-six. She was an amazing woman. It takes
a special person to marry a baseball scout. She had to carry so
much of the load. It's been tough since she died, but this is my
work, my job, my vocation. She's now an angel who helps me. The
boys are older now, so that helps, but I wish Christine were here
to help with the two teenage girls. I sometimes think it's harder to
deal with them than it is to find a hard-hitting shortstop.

The hard-hitting shortstop … the Holy Grail of baseball scout-
ing. That's what has drawn him here today. Christine understood
that, and their children do as well. They also know that John is very

good at his job, and the White Sox have scores of players in their system to offer up as proof.

John dials home on his cell phone and his elder daughter picks up. They are just watching a movie, she says, and ordering a pizza. Electronic kisses and hugs are exchanged, and John goes back to work.

The stands are now pretty much full. Like everyone else, John stands for "The Star-Spangled Banner" and then sits down again for the announcement of the starting lineups.

The game gets underway and John locks his eyes on Donny. He's impressed. Donny hits a tough pitch for a hard single, and John makes a note in his journal. This is a good test because the pitcher Donny is facing is one of the best in their age group.

Sometimes a player's statistics can be misleading. If they play against weak competition all the time, they hit lots of home runs, but they aren't useful home runs. I have to evaluate how a player will perform against pitchers with velocity and breaking balls that move. So I look for games where they face good competition. Sometimes coaches will organize all-star games as well to put everyone to the test.

In the fifth inning John observes something else he came here hoping to see: a big mistake. The batter hits a soft ground ball toward Donny, who picks it up. When he sees that the batter is almost at first base, Donny panics; instead of just holding on to the ball, he rushes a throw. He throws too hard, without a proper grip, and the ball flies over the first baseman's head and into the outfield. The runner sprints around the bases and makes it all the way to third.

The crowd lets out a long sigh. It's a close game, and that sort of thing could cost them a victory. But John narrows his eyes and watches Donny closely. The young player doesn't hang his head,

and that's a good thing. He points to himself as if to say to his teammates, "My fault, sorry." Donny knows he rushed his mechanics instead of trusting his instincts. Then he quickly settles himself back into position and waits for the next play. John smiles.

I need to see how players deal with adversity. Baseball is game of failure. The best hitters only get a hit every three times at the plate. Everyone makes errors in the field. To be great, you have to be humble and you have to be able to forget your mistakes – and your successes.

In making draft choices, the chain of command is pretty long. The team wants as many people as possible to have input into a potentially multi-million-dollar investment. John says, "First you contact your area supervisor and submit a report on the player. Then you also get paperwork completed on the health history of the player, the ability to sign the player, including information about agents. Then you do some follow-up on the background of the player. I also make sure I see the player again and get a chance to sit down with him to get to know him. We'll keep in contact and I'll make sure I know anything and everything I can about him. Then I make sure everyone else in the chain knows that as well."

The next batter hits the ball right at Donny. He jumps in the air and makes an acrobatic leaping catch. The inning is over, and John is convinced. This kid is the real deal. Tomorrow he'll call the White Sox head scout and tell him the team should add Donny to their draft list.

That's not the end of the job, though.

Sometimes you have to fight for your player. The top two or three players in the draft list are a given. Everyone has seen them. My job is often to fight for the lower picks. Let's say I've seen someone they've never heard of. I have to convince them that I'm right, that this player has the stuff to become a major-leaguer. That's why I study them so much. My reputation is at stake, as well as their future.

John scouted Mark Buehrle, who pitched a perfect game for Chicago in 2009.

John has a reputation that gets the Sox to listen to him, and he's earned it with years of hard work and good tips.

One of John's biggest success stories is pitcher Mark Buehrle. John saw him as a skinny left-handed pitcher with some skill but great character. He told the Sox they should take a chance, and they sent more scouts to take a look. They saw what John saw and the Sox drafted him in the thirty-eighth round. That's low, but it still meant that Buehrle was part of the system. He made the team by the time he was twenty-one, and at twenty-eight Mark pitched a no-hitter and helped the White Sox win the World Series.

Along the way, John and Mark kept in touch, exchanging Christmas cards and such. Then came July 23, 2009. Mark pitched a perfect game: twenty-seven batters faced, twenty-seven outs.

I cried. I'm a bit of a marshmallow, but it was like watching one of my children being born. It was exciting and moving. People started calling me during the game, making sure I was watching "my guy."

I was. It was a sign that all the hard work, the sacrifice was worth it, not just for me but for Mark too. If I hadn't seen him and then recommended him, he might not have made the major leagues.

Back on the high school field the game is ending. Donny has made two more hits and his team is up by five runs. The final batter hits a sky-high pop-up. Donny settles under it and calmly makes the catch. The crowd stands and cheers. Donny smiles and jogs off the field, handing out high-fives to his teammates and his coaches along the way. He waves to his parents and then makes his way to the dugout.

John will try to catch him in a few more games and will eventually introduce himself to Donny. He looks at his watch. Not tonight. He has another game to catch tomorrow, in Nevada. It could just as easily be in Colorado or Utah. He wants to get there tonight, settle into another in a long list of anonymous motel rooms, and get some sleep. He hopes he'll have time to call home again, to wish everyone goodnight.

It's not an easy life. Every morning I walk to my car and I debate whether or not to turn the ignition key. All the miles I drive, the long days … are they worth it? But then I think, Maybe today is the day I find the next hidden gem. Maybe today is the day I scout a player who'll make it to the bigs, and I can help him realize his dream. *Every day that I start with that thought I get in the car, turn the key, and drive a long time. I still love it.*

Chapter 11

POMPOMS AND POWER

This team leader choreographs an all-out athletic effort.
Job: head cheerleader
Location: Dallas, TX
Sport: football

Kelli Finglass

Kelli Finglass takes a deep breath. She adjusts her outfit and tries to channel her nervous energy into concentrating on her performance. She's been at the stadium for hours already, getting ready for the big game, which is now just a few minutes away. Time to get her game face on. She stands up and gets ready to assemble the team.

Kelli takes a moment to look around. The team's new locker room at Cowboys Stadium in Dallas still amazes her. It's huge, bright, and packed with the latest high-tech equipment. There are weight machines and stationary bikes for training, and a carpeted floor to cushion painful feet after a full day of all-out athletic effort. Pictures of the greats past and present cover the walls. Each member of the team has her own locker, electrical outlet, and mirror. It's a huge upgrade from their old home, Texas Stadium, where more than thirty women had to line up for the four or five outlets and single mirror.

"All right, girls," Kelli says. "Time for the last-minute fluff-and-puff, a prayer, and then we hit the field." Kelli Finglass is in charge of one of the most famous teams in the world, the Dallas Cowboys Cheerleaders.

"Fluff-and-puff" is a phrase I coined that refers to last-minute touch-ups before a stage call. Check your hair and makeup – millions of people are going to see you on TV and live at the stadium, so you'd better look good.

Looking good is definitely part of the Dallas Cowboys Cheerleaders' mystique. That's where the mirrors and the numerous outlets come in handy. "Getting your game face on" for a football player means gritting your teeth and smearing on eye-black to reduce the glare of the sun or the lights. It means a lot more for the DCCs: makeup, lipstick, hair spray. And all that has to stand up to hours of sweat, dancing, and whatever conditions Mother Nature has decided to throw at you on game day.

Kelli knows every part of the routine intimately. She doesn't just lead the team; she danced on the sidelines as a Dallas Cowboys Cheerleader for five years.

I grew up in East Texas watching the Dallas Cowboys and admiring the cheerleaders. I was nineteen years old and a dance major at Texas Christian University when I heard an ad for the auditions on the radio and I thought, I'd like to try that. So I did. There were a thousand women lined up in the parking lot the day I showed up. I was one of the lucky ones who made it in my first year of auditioning, and my life was changed forever.

The Cheerleaders have been performing on the sidelines of Cowboys games for more than thirty years. Kelli often gets asked why there are no male members of the team.

There actually were male cheerleaders in the 1960s. Back then, both male and female cheerleaders were selected from local high school students. Their style was more collegiate in nature, with team cheers and stunts. Then, in 1972, we introduced a new style of cheerleader who was sexy and graceful, so dance routines replaced the cheers and stunts. Megaphones and pleated skirts were replaced by go-go boots and short shorts.

> Making it onto the cheerleading squad on your first try isn't easy, to say the least. Every year more than six hundred hopefuls show up for open auditions for the Dallas Cowboys Cheerleaders – and that includes returning DCCs as well. There's even a TV reality show that follows the progress of the auditions.

There are, of course, critics. They charge that the cheerleaders are eye candy, spending most of the game smiling and waving their pompoms. This stigma has dogged the women who take these jobs. A pretty face is indeed part of the job requirements (the Dallas Cowboys Cheerleaders sell an annual swimsuit calendar, after all), but Kelli says the critics are selling the DCCs short.

When the DCCs first hit the field in the early 1970s, Cowboys manager Tex Schramm actually hired professional models to attract more male fans to the games. But he found that the models tired quickly and didn't really have the athletic skill or training to do the job well.

The team was soon looking for people with a more athletic and artistic background – people such as Kelli.

We have a very diverse fitness program that includes cardio dance, boot camp, and yoga. The rehearsals and conditioning workouts are grueling, but they give the cheerleaders the stamina they need to perform for four continuous hours on the field.

Injuries are common because the dance routines are complex. Performance is one of the keystones of the job, and that means high kicks, jumps, splits, and spins that would make gymnasts gasp. And the performance must go on as long as the game lasts.

If a cheerleader gets injured, she visits the Dallas Cowboys trainer and an orthopedic doctor. The nature of the injury will determine how long she will need to rest and recover. She will remain on the squad but will not perform until the doctor releases her to do so.

Two of the cheerleaders are too injured to join today's game. Kelli goes over and hugs them, telling them they'll be back soon. Then she calls all the cheerleaders together in the middle of the room.

Cheerleading can be a dangerous sport. More than twenty thousand cheerleaders are sent to the emergency room each year. And one study by the National Center for Catastrophic Injuries discovered forty-four fatalities from cheerleading between 1982 and 2007. It's not surprising, given the athletic demands on the (mostly) women who perform at games.

The thirty-six cheerleaders stand up and shake out their muscles to calm their nerves. To keep them loose, Kelli invites them to tell some jokes or crank up the locker room music. It's a trick she's learned from all those years spent driving from game to game and event to event.

One of our senior veterans, Tandra Cromer, told the same joke on every bus ride for five years in a row. It became such a tradition for us, and although we could all quote the joke and anticipate the

punch line, we still wanted to hear Tandra deliver her famous donkey joke on the bus driver's microphone … every bus ride, every trip, for five years!

Soon it's time for a final moment of reflection and preparation. Kelli leads them all in a pre-game prayer. Gathering in the middle of the locker room, the cheerleaders bow their heads.

Together we all pray the Lord's Prayer. It's a tradition that goes back before I joined the team.

They pray for a good performance and for no injuries. They also pray for warm weather. Thank goodness today's game is in Dallas.

We had an event in Spokane, Washington, once. It was freezing! Far and away the coldest I've ever been.

There's not much fabric involved in the official cheerleader uniform. Each woman wears short shorts, a cropped blouse, a star-spangled vest, and stylized cowboy boots. The costumes are tailor-made for each cheerleader, who is expected to treasure hers for the season.

The prayer finished, Kelli claps her hands and tells the cheerleaders, "Let's rock 'n' roll!" Kelli has become a mentor to the team. She's led them on and off the field for nearly twenty years, but she still gets the jitters as the cheerleaders prepare to head down the tunnel to the field.

Although cold weather is no fun for the lightly clad cheerleaders, warm weather can sometimes bring out the wacky in the fans. Kelli says, "The weirdest thing I've seen was a streaker. It was at a game in the 1990s. We looked up and a naked guy was running across the field! It happened fast and was obviously unexpected. Security had him on the ground in seconds and he was removed immediately, thank goodness."

I remember my first tunnel walk – it was amazing. But I think I remember my last performance more distinctly. I'd been a member of the team for five years and it was very emotional. Of course, it is very different for me as a director, but I still find it very exciting to watch each rookie take her first walk down the tunnel and onto the field.

As the women make their way down the tunnel, the roar of the crowd rumbles toward them like thunder. They rush out onto the field to a standing ovation, as loud as the players will receive when they run out in a few minutes. The music blares through the speakers, filling the stadium with loud *boom-boom-boom* echoes. The fans clap to the beat and the cheerleaders form a long chorus line, dancing and kicking in unison. The music is a perfect fit. Kelli, who is standing at the fifty-yard line, smiles.

I notice music all the time, everywhere I am – in the car, at restaurants, on the radio, in the hair salon. I look for music with energy and orchestration. I specifically pay attention to the beats per minute and the brass and percussion in each song, for DCC momentum.

Finding great tunes is just one of the many jobs that Kelli does in organizing the team. Besides the music, she also handles appearances at special events and merchandising. The first Dallas Cowboys Cheerleaders line of Barbie dolls was one of her pet projects. During the game she's just like a coach, watching every detail to make sure her game plan – worked out with choreographer Judy Trammell – is followed to a tee.

I really don't get to watch the football. During the game I am walking around the field making notes into a recorder on everything from tattered pompoms to scuffed-up boots and choreography. I am also making notes about the music and watching to see what the fans react to, since we produce our halftime shows.

The Cowboys are doing well on the field, and the cheerleaders also keep the crowd pumped, dancing to the music during every available break, moving from section to section so that everyone gets a chance to join the fun.

Kelli knows that the cheerleaders are as much a team as the men on the field who are wearing their own costumes of plastic helmets and spandex pants. The women grow very close over the season and over the years together. It's a glamorous life in many ways, but Kelli knows it involves sacrifices as well.

Our days not in uniform often include homework, chores, and

struggles to balance schedules. All of our cheerleaders are either in college or working. Being a Dallas Cowboys Cheerleader is a full-time commitment, but it is part-time pay.

The game ends with the Cowboys losing. The cheerleaders fare better, however. There are no injuries, no major incidents, and the squad is performing at top speed. They continue to rally the crowd as the teams leave the field, some of the players limping.

Cheerleaders make a difference in the presentation of the game and contribute to the magic and energy of the Dallas Cowboys football experience. I think they add a wow factor that makes any game memorable.

You have to love it to do it. Kelli has grown up in this world, and she definitely loves it. It's a world she hopes she can continue to share with millions of fans.

The footsteps that I would hope my daughter will follow are all the right steps that I took along the way, and I hope that she will also have significant people who will influence her in a positive way. My wish for her is that she will find what she is passionate about and that she will be proud of my contributions. Maybe she'll even come to think of her mom as cool … she is a preteen now! But, really, a life full of fun and laughter is what we all want.

Chapter 12

THE MUSIC MAN

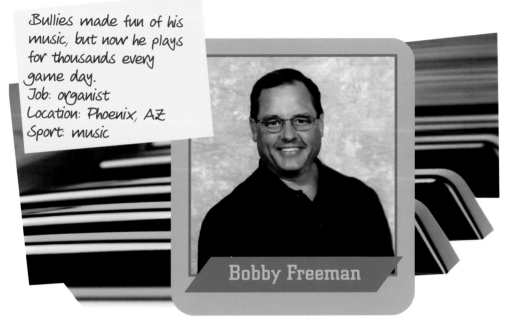

Bullies made fun of his music, but now he plays for thousands every game day.
Job: organist
Location: Phoenix, AZ
Sport: music

Bobby Freeman

It's the mid-1960s in Cleveland. Bobby Freeman is in fourth grade, and it's show-and-tell at school. Most kids are bringing in toys or games, or maybe dead frogs – cool stuff.

Bobby has brought his grandfather's accordion. It's possibly the uncoolest instrument in the musical world, but it's special to him. Bobby plays it for the class: the theme from the TV show *Batman*. He finishes with a flourish. The nun who is teaching the class claps her hands. She loves it, and she quickly makes Bobby visit the rest of the classes in the school to play the same song for everyone.

It doesn't take a fan of *The Simpsons* to know what happens next. The 1960s Cleveland versions of Jimbo, Nelson, and the rest chase him after school, teasing him and trying to grab the accordion. Bobby feels hurt, both physically and emotionally.

He thought they'd like the music, so he's surprised. But Bobby

Seventeen-year-old Bobby at his Hammond Organ in 1973.

loves playing music more than anything and he's determined to keep it up, bullies or no bullies. He brings his accordion to school again and again, and he learns how to run home as fast as possible.

Today Bobby Freeman is the organist for Major League Baseball's Arizona Diamondbacks.

I think I made the right choices. I'm not sure what the bullies are doing now, but I bet they aren't as happy as I am.

He smiles. It's been a long trip from fourth grade to Chase Field in downtown Phoenix, but a great trip. He's one of the more popular figures in the city. Everyone says a cheery hello to him as he makes his way from the front door of the field, up the long hallways to his perch high above in left field. No one bullies him now.

I do a lot of school visits and tell kids my story. I want them to see

that persistence and confidence are what are important. Yes, it's hard to stick with something when it's not the "in" thing, but don't give up if it's something you love.

Bobby Freeman grew up in a tough neighborhood in Cleveland. He was smaller than most of the other boys, and not as interested in sports as he was in music. He says he did love bowling, and became pretty good at that, but music was always the most important thing. Growing up, Bobby learned how to play the piano, the accordion, the harmonica, and the violin, and learned how to play them well.

My family came from a German background. Music is a kind of international language, so that's how we communicated. Well, great music and great food always went together growing up. We would have big family gatherings and we would play around the kitchen table. It was amazing.

Bobby figures that part of the bullying over the accordion was because it was seen as an ethnic instrument, as un-American in some way. But there were plenty of people who loved the music and wanted to celebrate traditional instruments, culture, and songs.

There was a local TV talent show that featured polka music. I tried again and again to get on and I finally made it. I almost blew it, though.

He was so nervous that he played the song too quickly.

They had budgeted about four minutes for the song, and I finished it in two. This was live TV, so we had to fill the time by talking. Luckily I could do that too, and the host loved the fact that here

was this young kid who could really play well, so they asked me back. I timed my music better after that.

Bobby became a semi-regular and decided this was going to be his career. He played music all the time, in as many different styles and on as many different instruments as he could. He also saved up his money and – with some help from his parents – when he was ten, he splurged on the instrument that would change his life. Bobby bought a Hammond organ. The cost: a whopping one thousand dollars. He soon mastered it, and his timing couldn't have been better.

Roller skating was a big thing when I was growing up. I used to spend hours at the roller rink watching, and especially listening. They had live organ music in those days. When I turned fifteen, I thought, I can do that, so I applied at the local rink. The rest, as they say, is history.

Bobby was playing live music for a live audience, and they wanted music they could skate to and groove to. A regular beat was a must, so Bobby learned how to keep very strict time. He also learned how to change the mood and speed of the action with different tempos. Some songs got the skaters moving and swaying; some got them cheering.

The bullying stopped too. It had kept up for years, but it's amazing how they shut up when they find out you're getting paid.

Music was his life. Bobby worked weekends in a music store. He played nights at the rink and filled in the rest of his schedule with as many other gigs as he could find, at restaurants and nightclubs and anywhere people wanted dance music. He even started doing better in school.

I had never liked school much before. I always felt it was institutionalized. The bullying made me want to stay away as well. But as I grew up and did more and more music I started to grow more confident. I even used some of the money I was earning to get a tutor, who helped me get pretty good grades.

One other incident decided Bobby's future around this time, and it was nasty. As well as making his way as a musician, Bobby had become a pretty good bowler, a sport he had dabbled in all his life. He was starting to win at tournaments, but he would have to scale back his music if he was going to improve at bowling.

One winter day I got into a really bad accident while sledding down a hill, and I had to spend weeks in hospital in a body cast. That ended any athletic aspirations I had. Thank goodness I had music and hadn't screwed up my arms and fingers.

By the time Bobby had recovered enough to go back to work, roller skating was starting to undergo a transformation. Rinks were moving from live music to recorded music. The writing was on the wall – Bobby needed to find a new outlet for his career. Then a friend told him about the growing ballroom dancing scene in southern Arizona.

I said, "Why not?" I had played lots of other venues and knew how to keep perfect time. I could play almost any type of music on any type of instrument. So I took the leap and left Cleveland. My friend was right. There was a growing demand for organists, and I found work right away.

He found more than just work. He also found his wife, Charlene.

Bobby in his perch high above left field.

She played the piano and loved the same music as Bobby. They married in 1990, but it wasn't until three years later that Bobby first heard Charlene's voice. She was singing the words to a song that he was trying to learn.

I thought, Wow, I didn't know you could sing! *Charlene then began an unexpected singing career alongside me, and she and I have appeared together ever since.*

It was Charlene who got Bobby his big break playing the organ for a sports team, and it's no surprise that it was for a baseball team.

If there's one thing Arizona is known for, it's sunny weather. This makes it an ideal place for baseball; there are few rainouts – very few. Bobby had gone to see Cleveland Indians games when he was kid, and he had also played some baseball.

I was good at stealing bases. Did I mention that I learned to run fast to get away from the bullies?

Bobby loved the tradition of the old Cleveland ball field – the grass, the hot dogs with Stadium Mustard, and the sound of the organ. No matter how badly the team lost (and they lost a lot), the organ music kept the crowd lively. So Bobby knew the game well.

Bobby was excited when he and his family were invited to attend a minor-league baseball game in Phoenix, where Charlene was setting up a group event for her employer.

She mentioned to people who ran the baseball team that I played the organ. There was an instant invitation to have me play at the game the night of the company event.

Bobby stresses the importance of Stadium Mustard. Every sports stadium has its own specialties. Chicken wings are a staple in Buffalo, of course, although the nachos at the old Memorial Auditorium were great too. Former player Boog Powell and his ribs are a staple of any visit to Baltimore. And in Cleveland it's hot dogs with Stadium Mustard. Astronaut Don Thomas even requested specially packaged Stadium Mustard for his trip on the space shuttle.

Bobby showed up for the Firebirds game, and again fate played a hand in his life.

It started raining. Suddenly there were sixty-five-hundred fans who didn't have a baseball game to watch. I started playing every sing-along song I knew, and the crowd really got into it. That day secured my place as an organist. It hadn't been a tryout situation, but because of the rain I got to show the team's owners what I could really do.

It was like being back at the roller rink but without the dancing (or the roller skates) – just a crowd hungry for melody and a good

beat. Seven years after Bobby's debut, a major-league team asked him if he'd like to do some big-league games. It would be a bit of a commute, however, because the team was the San Diego Padres.

I hadn't really thought of sports as my future. I was still getting lots of work doing the dance circuit, but I said I could do some of the games. It's a great city, but I needed to do a lot of flying. So I started doing games here and there, but it was still a part-time gig.

This was all happening in the mid-1990s, when baseball teams were looking to bring back some of the traditions of the game, including organ music. Bobby learned a lot with the Firebirds and the Padres.

You have to know what music is proper for the way the game is going. You don't want to play something that fires up the crowd when the other team is batting. You also don't want to play rah-rah music if your team is down several runs out there.

Eventually the news broke that Phoenix was going to get its own team, the Diamondbacks. They were going to build a new stadium. It would have a retractable roof for those scorching summer days, and a grass field. And it would have an organ. The Diamondbacks asked Bobby to join the team.

It was a lot closer to home, but I was still committed to some games in San Diego. It was a challenging situation for a while because I was the organist for competing teams. I eventually chose the Diamondbacks, and I am part of that team.

He's a bona fide celebrity along with the players. Visit Bobby at

a game and you'll see how true that is. It takes about ten minutes to stroll from the employees' entrance to the top tier and Bobby's organ perch. That is, if you're not Bobby. It can take him a long time to make his way to his "play station," as he calls it. Everybody says hi to him and he says hi to everybody – the team's office staff, security, players. Bobby stops and chats with all of them, about everything from the weather and how the team is doing to what music he should play during the game. If he has guests along he introduces them to everyone, including the players. He also stops and shows them the memorabilia that cover the walls.

Once Bobby steps out of the elevator into the seating area, he's approached by fans asking for autographs, especially kids.

Kids just love the music. Sometimes I get them to sit down at the stadium organ and play for a bit before the game begins. Because I was a kid who loved music, and that wasn't always the popular thing, I try to take time to encourage kids and make them see how much fun music can be.

Bobby takes that message out on the road as well. He and the team mascot, Baxter, visit schools, libraries, and community centers around Arizona. They host reading clubs and anti-bullying seminars.

Once the game begins, though, it's all business. Bobby turns off

> Bobby doesn't play all the sound effects at the game. There's a DJ as well, who handles the music for when different players come up to bat. The players choose these snippets and they are played from discs. To make sure they don't step on each other's toes, Bobby and the DJ work out a rough script for the game, which includes such things as public service announcements and ads. They stay in touch throughout the game by using headsets and a kind of code. If Bobby says "the dance," it means he's going to play the theme music from Zorba the Greek. If the game operations director calls for a "fantastic," it's Bobby's cue to play one of the Diamondbacks' "big rally songs," like "Charge!" At this point the huge HDTV screen in center field, along with the LED ribbon board that runs from foul pole to foul pole in the ballpark, will display a big graphic CHARGE!

his emotions and immerses himself in the ebb and flow of the action on the field.

I can't be distracted. If I'm not watching I might play a happy song when the other team is at bat. That's not a good thing. Or I might play when a pitcher is delivering the ball or a batter is getting ready to swing.

Bobby and Charlene Freeman hoisting the Diamondbacks' World Series Trophy.

Bobby probably watches the game more closely than anyone else in the stadium, with the possible exception of the managers. If there are two outs and the Diamondbacks are up to bat, he'll play something like "Hava Nagila," which always gets the crowd clapping. If Arizona is down a run with runners on base, he'll play "Charge!" to get the fifty thousand fans on hand to yell together. But some details are more subtle.

I watch to see if the umpire has signaled to the batboy for more baseballs. It means he doesn't have any left to replace balls that go into the crowd or get scuffed. From experience I know that if the batter hits a foul ball, there will be a twenty-five-second pause while those new baseballs are delivered. That's when I can play a good long rally chant.

Bobby is watching for that from more than five hundred feet away. That care, that minute understanding of the game, has made him the go-to guy for all the Phoenix sports teams – baseball, hockey, and basketball.

I'm the answer to a trivia question. I'm the only guy to play for every level of sports in the state. I've played for the Firebirds, Diamondbacks, the Coyotes, the minor-hockey Roadrunners, and the Suns!

Bobby still plays for dancers and has even played live music for silent movies. Variety keeps him going. That and the memory of that boy in fourth grade who just wanted to play music – and stuck with it – bullies or no bullies.

I tell kids, whatever you want to be, it will require hard work, respect for yourself and for others, and making good choices along the way. I'm very lucky to wake up every day saying, "Take me out to the ballgame!"

Chapter 13

"GOD BLESS AMERICA"

Losing both legs just
pushed him to incredible
heights.
Job: tenor
Location: New York, NY
Sports: baseball and hockey

Ronan Tynan

With apologies to a recent advertising campaign you may have seen, Ronan Tynan is quite possibly the most interesting man in the world. He has been a world-class athlete, despite losing both legs in an accident. He was the first amputee to be accepted into medical school in his native Ireland. One of the most celebrated tenors in the world, he sings "God Bless America," Irving Berlin's love song to the United States. And he has been a huge part of the baseball experience in New York City and the hockey experience in Buffalo.

I have grown to love baseball and hockey. I played cricket and rugby as a kid and I loved horses too, but now that I live in the United States I have become a huge Yankees and Sabres fan.

The players are huge Ronan Tynan fans as well. In Buffalo, the Sabres players have "The will is inside you" posted on their locker room wall and printed on T-shirts. It's a quote from Ronan, whose personal story has inspired them.

This is Ronan's story: He was born in Kilkenny, Ireland, making – in his mother Therese's words – a "ferocious racket." The priest told his mother that with lungs like that he would surely be a singer someday.

The doctor was more worried about young Ronan's legs. They were too short, his feet were turned at an angle, and he had only three toes on each foot. The doctors diagnosed phocomelia, a disability of the limbs, and said that he might never walk.

Ronan's legs hurt constantly and he spent much of his first three years in hospital. His mother and father refused to accept the doctors' gloomy predictions and eventually brought him home. Therese Tynan worked hard to make sure that young Ronan got special braces to help him walk. Rather than hide his difference, she made him wear shorts to school just like the other boys.

My mum in particular would never let me hide behind my disability. "What's there to hide?" she said to me. And she also wanted people to have to face it up front – no comments behind my back. I was who I was. There were no excuses, and no need for them either.

"The will is inside you. You just have to bring it out.... The team player gets the result. Not one man. If the team is together in thought and spirit, then you have an army." These are the words that Ronan Tynan spoke to the Buffalo Sabres before one of his first games in Buffalo. The Sabres adopted this statement as their inspirational motto.

Ronan has sung at state events such as the funeral of former US president Ronald Reagan and to US army troops in Afghanistan. He has sung at the White House for presidential balls and St. Patrick's Day parties. He has also sung "New York, New York" to open the Belmont Stakes horse race and entertained at the eightieth birthday party of former US president George H.W. Bush and the wedding of former New York mayor Rudy Giuliani.

Edmond Tynan told his son that he could do anything. He also introduced him to one of his first passions: music.

My father and I would sing to the cows when we milked them. I think, like all romantic females, they loved a strong man with a good voice. And we got better milk too.

Above all else, Ronan loved being active. Maybe spurred on by the memory of those long years confined to a hospital bed, he yearned to be outdoors and on the move all the time. Some sports were closed to him, but he learned to ride horses and fell in love with the freedom and speed that riding gave him. Ignoring the pain in his legs and the discomfort of the braces, he rode around the countryside whenever he could. He was a natural, and soon he was competing throughout Ireland.

Ronan also loved something even faster: motorcycles. It was a motorcycle accident that eventually caused him to lose his legs.

I was riding down a highway in Ireland when a car cut me off. I had nowhere else to go, so I slammed into the car. It injured my legs and worsened some problems I'd been having with my back – problems that stemmed from my disability. I chose to have both legs amputated.

He was barely twenty years old. The doctors fitted him with pros-thetics – artificial lower legs – and told him to take it easy for a while. How did Ronan react? As you might expect of a man with such energy for life, he wanted to get moving immediately. So he went dancing.

That was maybe not the best decision, but I went dancing with a

young lady for hours and hours. The sutures hadn't even set, and they started bleeding. I ended up right back in hospital.

But there was no keeping Ronan down for long. A self-described sponge for experience, he made two decisions. One was to look for a new way to stay active in sports, and the second was to come up with a better way to build prosthetics.

In 1984, just two years after his accident, Ronan competed in the Paralympic Games, and again in 1988. He dominated the competition.

I was particularly interested in the discus. I studied technique like crazy and practiced as much as I could. I threw it so far they tested me to see if I was taking banned substances!

He wasn't, as extensive tests proved. This was welcome news for his mother when he called to tell her about his win. She actually let out a long sigh of relief when Ronan told her about the clean bill of health he'd received from the anti-doping officials.

> The Paralympic Games are games for athletes with disabilities; they run parallel with the Olympics. Many of the athletes are former soldiers who have lost limbs in wars. In 1948 a man named Ludwig Guttmann organized a sporting event for veterans of the Second World War who suffered from spinal injuries. That was held in England. More countries joined the movement, and the first Paralympic Games were held in Rome in 1960. Four hundred athletes took part. Today the Paralympics welcome more than three thousand athletes.

My own mother had been worried! That tells you how good I was. I had to laugh, but I kept on winning.

In his career, Ronan went on to win eighteen gold medals and set fourteen world records, some of which stand to this day. At the same time he was doing research into his other vocation, medicine.

As he was killing the competition, Ronan was also pursuing the healing arts. He was accepted into the National College of Physical Education out of high school, the first disabled student to achieve that. He went on to study orthopedics and earned a degree from prestigious Trinity College.

He was experimenting with better prosthetics that would have more flexibility and strength and that could even store power to help ease the fatigue of the remaining part of the arm or leg. Ronan was both designer and, often, chief guinea pig. As an athlete he could test the extremes of the new designs. If they could survive the pounding he put them through, then they would be more than durable enough for everyday use.

Music was always there. Ronan heard the Irish national anthem played after his gold medal wins, and he sang along with the fans at big sporting events.

Ronan Tynan once borrowed a competitor's foot to win a race. He had broken the foot off his own artificial leg, so he asked the guy next to him if he could borrow one. He went on to win the race, then handed the foot back!

It's not just a North American tradition. We would sing "Ireland's Call" before big rugby matches back home. The song is sung by fans in both Northern Ireland and the Republic of Ireland, and it's seen as a unifying song for all the Irish. It's not a national anthem per se, but it was a national anthem to us, and we sang it lustily.

Eventually, as for all athletes, it was time for Ronan to retire. He left his medals on his mom and dad's mantelpiece, graduated from university, and settled down into a private medical practice. But he still sang whenever he could, in pubs or when helping his parents milk the cows.

One day his father gave him a call. There was a new talent show

on TV, called *Go for It*, and they were looking for undiscovered stars.

I was delivering babies, not looking at singing as a living, but I told my dad I would try. He always loved me so much and really pushed me to follow my passions. I started taking lessons and found out that I loved it even more than I thought I would.

Natural talent alone isn't enough. Ronan knew that lesson well from everything he had already achieved. And now he applied it to singing. It's hard work to train your voice. It takes hours of practice to learn to sing so clearly that the audience can hear each word. You have to learn the music as well, of course, and how to match your pitch to the instruments or the other people singing. Ronan threw himself wholeheartedly into the effort.

He won the *Go for It* competition. Then, a year later, he won an international operatic competition in France. Not long after that he was appearing in professional opera performances and choral concerts. He wasn't a practicing doctor for much longer.

I often say to people that not taking a risk is the biggest risk in life. Because if you don't try then you'll never know what you can do.

Ronan's singing caught the ear of a music producer in the United States. He was putting together a group of singers called the Irish Tenors for a series of concerts and TV shows. Ronan was Irish, and he was a great tenor. He was asked to join.

I did that for four successful years. We toured all over the world. I fell in love with the US, and especially New York City. This is a country that rewards and holds up people who work hard and do well. I decided to go solo and stay in the Big Apple.

Ronan found work in cabarets, stage shows, and concert halls. He also produced best-selling CDs. One day, a chance encounter at a restaurant introduced him to a new audience: sports fans.

I was watching a game on TV and I started chatting to the man next to me. It turned out he was with the New York Yankees. He asked me to sing at a game. It ended up being the Yankees hosting their arch-rivals from Boston. I sang "God Bless America." The Yankees won and I was asked back.

Ronan's rendition took on extra meaning after the terrorist attacks of September 11, 2001. When baseball resumed, he took to the field to sing the song for all the victims who had died when the planes hit the World Trade Center towers.

It was heartbreaking. I knew people who had died in the towers. Those terrorists had no respect for human life. I was crying inside, but I needed to control my emotions to sing.

People in the crowd and watching on TV knew this was a special moment. They knew Ronan was singing to declare that New Yorkers would bounce back. It was a moment that was not confined to just a baseball game, or even to the traditions of American sports.

Some people have wondered why Ronan doesn't sing "The Star-Spangled Banner," the official US national anthem. But he feels that only an American citizen should have that honor. He has applied for citizenship, but his request has been held up for a while by red tape.

Despite the emotional force of Ronan's voice, his seventh-inning tradition isn't without its critics. Most performers sing only the final verse of the song, the one that begins with the words "God bless America" and has the familiar melody. Ronan sings the opening

Ronan enjoys singing anywhere, anytime.

verse as well, which takes about an extra minute or so. Some critics suggest that this gives the home team an advantage in the bottom of the seventh inning. The argument is that home team batters get a little extra rest while the opposing pitcher gets too much rest. This makes Ronan fume.

I don't sing the "long version." I sing the song the way Irving Berlin wrote it. For anyone who thinks that gives a pitcher "frozen shoulder" ... Let's just say that I'm a doctor, and that's absolute nonsense!

Clearly the fans outnumber the critics. Ronan has been asked to sing at sporting events all over the world, including a big outdoor hockey game in Buffalo in snowy January. Ronan has performed on many of the most famous stages in the world, but he still gets a special thrill when he steps onto the field at a baseball diamond or before the crowd in Buffalo.

It's a privilege. Just think of Lou Gehrig, the great Yankee, who gave one of the most emotional speeches in sports history at Yankee Stadium. He was dying, yet he stood at a microphone on the field and told the fans that he was the luckiest man in the world. I have stood in that spot, and I respect that. I am a lucky man as well.

Some risks come with singing at sporting events. It can be cold and wet outside at a ballpark, or cold and dry inside an arena. The key, Ronan says, is good preparation … and faith.

I do at least thirty minutes of warm-ups. I start singing slowly, warming up my voice, being careful not to strain my vocal cords. It's just like being an athlete: a proper warm-up will help prevent injuries. By the time the game starts I should have my nice mellow voice working. After that, it's all in the hands of the man above!

Ronan credits his strong religious beliefs (he's a Roman Catholic) for his ability to never give up, to overcome the difficulties that life can throw your way.

I always say to young children who may face obstacles such as disabilities that there is always light coming into your life. Faith feeds that light. Forget about the problems that face you, learn to like yourself, have faith in a better you – and you can do anything.

Chapter 14

THE DETECTIVE

She looks for the joyful child in the eyes of the grown-up pro.
Job: journalist
Location: Toronto, ON
Sport: all of them!

Mary Ormsby

Mary Ormsby quickly pulls her car over to the side of the road. She's caught a glimpse of something out of the corner of her eye, something she tries to capture every day in her life as a sports journalist but rarely sees.

She turns off the ignition and climbs out from behind the wheel. She's supposed to be on her way downtown to catch the Toronto Raptors basketball team practice. But there's plenty of time for that.

There's a chill in the air and a slight wind is blowing, making the branches in the nearby woods sway. As multicolored leaves dance in the autumn breeze, Mary buttons her coat and walks closer to the trees. She peers between the trunks and then smiles. A group of schoolchildren is running a cross-country race through the woods.

There is such joy in the faces of those young boys and girls. They aren't earning big money or playing for Olympic medals. They are just having fun doing what they love.

Mary remembers that feeling from her childhood, when she was a star runner and then a volleyball player. She went on to play for Canada and win a volleyball scholarship at Ohio State University. For her, sports has always meant being active, being joyful.

Pro sports are so magnified, and there's great drama. But those small school or community track meets really sum up what sports means to me. I don't often report on them, but I just love to stop and watch them.

The last bunch of school kids passes the clearing in the trees and disappears into the woods. Mary pauses for one more moment and then checks her watch. She'll have to hurry, but she'll get to the Raptors practice on time. And this surprise encounter has given her a renewed passion for tonight's basketball game.

One of my first editors told me early on that sport is really all about people. The scores aren't always the important thing. I focus on other things.

This has proven to be an especially fruitful approach in the Internet age. People who want to know the score have many ways to find that out without waiting for the paper to arrive on their doorstep. A good sportswriter looks for ways to explain the game without relying on that information.

I'm writing for the next morning, so when I watch a game I ask

myself, "What is this game about?" Is it about a player who's com-
ing back from an injury? Is it about a veteran player who's looking
to win the big prize before retirement? Sometimes I'm looking for
glimpses of that little kid in the big pro player.

This approach has made Mary one of the most read and respected sportswriters in the business.

Mary has been covering sports for more than twenty years. She used her volleyball scholarship to get a top-notch journalism degree at Ohio State. She originally shied away from covering sports – it seemed like too familiar a world to her – but she landed a summer job with the local *Dayton Daily News* and was hooked.

> Mary covers games, but she also writes columns about other subjects, branching out to include everything from crime to culture. She's able to devote more time to developing stories away from the results.

I just love the friendliness of sports. You are surrounded by young
people all the time, and they have such energy. And the games are
always different and unpredictable. The endings of each story, each
season are always changing.

After that summer ended, Mary looked for full-time work back home in Toronto. This was in the early 1980s, when the world of sports journalism was largely what Mary describes as a "boys on the bus" male-dominated and chummy world. But the sports section was becoming an increasingly popular part of newspapers, and the papers were looking for new blood. Mary landed a job with the *Toronto Sun*, a sports-heavy tabloid.

They were looking for a "female," and they were very upfront
about that. I didn't care. I had my foot in the door.

Women had a hard time breaking into sports reporting. Most professional athletes are male, and not all of them accepted the idea of women walking into the locker room. Melissa Ludtke was one of the trailblazers. In the late 1970s she was trying to cover baseball playoff games for *Sports Illustrated*, but Major League Baseball commissioner Bowie Kuhn said that only men were allowed in the locker room. Ludtke and the magazine took Kuhn to court, and they won.

Mary's first assignment came right away. Her boss told her to interview Toller Cranston, one of the most talented, eccentric (and sometimes crusty) figure skaters in the history of the sport. He was in town for an extravaganza show – which was part skating, part theater.

I was nervous and I ended up walking into his dressing room while he was getting dressed. I was so shocked I just started asking him questions right on the spot. He was really nice and friendly, as it turned out, and I had my story.

Things haven't always gone so smoothly. Often in her early career Mary had football players yell insults at her when she was interviewing in the locker room. Some made rude gestures and uttered veiled threats. Mary refused to leave and continued working. She wrote about that in a 1985 column for her new employer, the *Toronto Star*, and got an apology from the Canadian Football League.

I had as much a right to be there as any other reporter. I refused to give in to the negative pressure. In a way it made me stronger. And I hope standing up to them made it easier for other women to become reporters.

It's certainly more common now to see women getting bylines in newspapers and also standing on the sidelines for live broadcasts. But it's still a largely male-dominated world. Mary says that being a woman often gives her a different perspective on the importance of sports.

My brothers, for example, grew up collecting baseball cards and memorizing stats. They wanted to be friends with these professional athletes. I'm not of that world. It makes me a bit of an outsider, and that can make it easier for me to view things from the outside, dispassionately.

Mary can say and write things that other writers might shy away from. When hockey player Dany Heatley crashed his car in a high-speed accident, resulting in the death of his teammate and friend Dan Snyder, Mary wrote a column calling him "a punk in a fast car." Many readers and hockey fans were angry, and they let her know it.

My job isn't all roses and chocolates. But you have to be willing to be critical when it's called for. The proof is in how you back it up. If you have credibility, then you can deal with the personal attacks. I know I can look the player in the face and stand by my words.

That "outsider" attitude also gives Mary freedom to question the conventional wisdom of many of her counterparts. She defended hockey bad boy Sean Avery after he made insulting comments about a former girlfriend and was suspended by his team, the Dallas Stars. He was drummed out of the NHL for months, and almost every sports columnist in the country supported the suspension.

Mary didn't agree with Avery's comments, but she wondered why the league was being so hypocritical. It allowed violence to thrive, handing out only tiny suspensions for the worst cheap shots, but then was coming down hard on something that was merely embarrassing. Was the NHL scoring cheap and easy public relations points?

Mary even made a call for Avery to be reinstated, and he did make his way back into the league with his old team, the New York Rangers. Mary says it helps to be an amateur "sideline psychologist,"

a skill she's gained from all her experience playing, watching, and reporting on sports.

That little child is still there, even in someone like Avery. He's a player who knows he's been given a second chance, and he still shows love for the game, for the excitement of playing. My job is to mine, to dig for that meaning and to show it in balance with the other parts of the story.

One of the amazing things about Mary, or any sportswriter, is that she can make these observations and analyses in such pressure-packed working conditions. Sporting events often end at around 10 p.m. The deadline for the first edition of the *Toronto Star* is 11 p.m.

In that situation you have to write as the game is going on, changing the details as the clock winds down. It actually helps, in a way, to focus on the story behind the game instead of the results. Let's say my story is going to be on a young basketball player like Andrea Bargnani. What he does in the game will change the details of the story but not the main part, which is the story of a young man from Italy who's trying to adjust to the North American game.

Mary gathers most of her quotes and tidbits of information from the morning practice. She also spends hours before the game at her desk or at home, sifting through sheets of stats and background information. As she says, you have to be ready for the unexpected because disaster can strike when you least expect it. Bargnani could get injured, for example, throwing Mary's planned story out the window. Sometimes something completely unexpected happens, like a player scoring six goals, and Mary has to change her focus completely. And sometimes other disasters strike.

The power has gone out just as I'm typing. I've spilled cola on my keyboard, completely frying it and my story – I've fried at least half a dozen computers like that. And more than once, if you can believe it, I've gone down to the locker room for post-game interviews and come back to find that somebody has stolen my computer bag.

What does she do in such situations? Mary says there are three possible reactions, and she usually goes through all of them.

First you panic. Then you wonder why you studied this in school. And then you get help.

Help comes from the team of co-workers surrounding her. Other reporters are covering the game too, some for the *Star* and some for rival papers. They might offer Mary their interview notes or computers – after they are done with their own stories, of course.

If all else fails, you write it down the best way you can by hand and then read it over the phone to an editor. They type it as you talk and you hope it all gets done in time to get into the paper.

There are always editors and copy editors back at the office ready to help catch spelling or factual errors in her copy. Sometimes they are there to argue with her about what she wants to write. Many of the senior editors have been covering sports for a long time, and they have long-standing opinions.

If you can defend your position it makes it a better story. You can't take anything for granted. We can get into some serious fights, but even that is helpful.

Mary says that everything that ends up in the paper is at least partly a team effort. Of course, it's her picture and name at the top of the story when the paper hits front porches early in the morning.

I've had regrets when I've read my stories the next morning, and the readers are always quick to point out anything they disagree with, but that's one of the things I love about sports – that back-and-forth. Sports means something.

Mary knows that meaning is sometimes buried in the business side of sports or in the competitive fires of the game. You can become cynical. You can get tired of covering game after game and sport after sport. But every once in a while, Mary glimpses the joy that she sees in school track meets peeking through in the pros. Maybe it's when an Olympic athlete wins an unexpected medal or when a player hoists the Stanley Cup or wins an NBA championship.

I have often thought about quitting sports reporting altogether, but then I'll see a young person shooting for the moon, trying to achieve something. In our world it's amazing to see young people with hope and excitement for life. I get a little teary-eyed some-times. Then I know that it's a privilege to do what I do.

Chapter 15

LIQUID GOLD

By watching athletes pee, he helps keep sport clean.
Job: doping control officer
Location: Boston, MA
Sport: rowing, judo, running, swimming ...

Scott Lowell

Scott Lowell walks toward the UPS facility. He is holding a Styrofoam box wrapped in what's called a "biological shipment bag." This odd package contains two sample bottles of warm urine.

Yes, urine. Scott is a doping control officer for the United States Anti-Doping Agency (USADA). He's just collected the pee from a member of the US rowing team at its training site in Cambridge, Massachusetts.

I have a list of athletes who live or train near my house. I get a note via our secure website saying, "You have two days to test a particular athlete," and I have to track them down and get them to provide a sample for me.

Many athletes cheat to try to gain an advantage in their given sport. Almost every Olympic Games sees at least one athlete kicked out or prevented from competing after being caught using banned substances, such as steroids. Each country has set up an anti-doping agency that tries to catch the dopers.

Scott has itineraries for all the athletes he might have to test. He knows where they train, where they live. And they can't know when he'll show up.

It can be tough for them. Sometimes I knock at their door at five in the morning and they have to give a sample for me. Sometimes I show up at their training site and they have just been working out for two hours. It's not easy to pee when you're dehydrated and exhausted.

The process is not for the easily embarrassed. To ensure the fairness and accuracy of the test, Scott can't let the athlete out of his sight, from the time he shows up until after he has collected the sample.

I have to make sure they can't secretly take a masking agent or even try to bolt to get away. When they give the sample, I need to see them nude from torso to mid-thigh. That makes sure they aren't using any devices to give me a clean or altered sample. Then I have to see the pee actually go into the cup. It was really awkward the first time I had to do that, but I've gotten used to it and the athletes aren't uncomfortable. This is part of their life.

Some cheaters will go to incredibly gross lengths to try to trick the tests. Some take clean pee (from someone who hasn't taken drugs) and put it in a catheter – a tube with a plastic sac attached. Then they insert the tube into their body and put the clean pee in their bladder. Yuck.

Scott has to follow detailed rules to ensure that the tests are fair. He starts off the whole process by asking the athlete a long list of questions. They sit down across from each other and Scott runs through the checklist.

I ask if they have taken any vitamins or nutritional supplements or used any glucocorticosteroids [medicines often used to treat severe asthma or allergic reactions] *or had any blood transfusions or used an inhaler recently. I also ask if they are on any prescription drugs that might show up on a test. This is of particular worry with Paralympic athletes, who are often on drugs to treat certain physical conditions. Athletes need to have written therapeutic-use exemptions from their sport federations to use any of those.*

The quiz is similar to questions people might have to answer when they give blood. Once that's over, Scott gives the athletes a choice of five collection vessels. They choose one and examine the individual bag that contains the vessel for any tampering, cracks, or dirt – anything that could spoil the test. Once the athlete is satisfied, he takes the vessel to the bathroom, rolls up his sleeves, and rinses his hands with just water (soap can contaminate the sample). Next the athlete will expose himself from mid-thigh to mid-torso so that when he is providing the sample, Scott can clearly witness it.

I don't touch anything until the samples are sealed. That way the athletes are the only ones who handle the samples,

If the athlete is female, Scott's wife witnesses the part where she actually provides the sample.

and we have each witnessed the whole process. Have you ever tried peeing in public? I often say that if the tables were turned and I had to pee in front of them, I don't know if I could do it.

Once the athlete has provided enough urine, the collection vessel is sealed by putting a cap on it.

The athletes have to provide at least ninety milliliters (about three ounces) of pee. They often have to drink water for a long time before they are able to generate enough of the necessary liquid, and

Scott has to wait with them the whole time. Sometimes he turns on the water taps to help out the athletes. Once they are done, Scott asks them to pour the sample into two separate bottles, giving the lab two samples to test. The athletes then seal the bottles and Scott has them place the vials in the Styrofoam package.

I give them a choice of boxes as well. They select one of three. This protects them and USADA. It keeps the tester at arm's length, so to speak. The vials are tamperproof once this is done, which means they can't be opened again until they reach the lab.

The samples are labeled A and B. The A sample is the primary sample that is used at the lab. The technicians look for traces of banned substances in the urine. Sometimes they find the drug itself, sometimes they find what are known as masking agents – substances athletes can take to hide the original drug in their system. The B sample is used only if there is a positive result. If both samples come back positive it is considered a positive test, and the athlete faces sanctions.

Scott takes a leftover drop from the sample after everything has been sealed into the two bottles. He places the drop on an instrument called a refractometer, to make sure the samples are dense enough to provide a good sample.

You want the sample to be nice and yellow. That means there's enough matter in there to test, although the color doesn't always matter. What is really important is that the sample is dense enough to go to the lab. The specific gravity needs to be at or above 1.005. That means it's heavier than distilled water [which is 1.000] and there's matter mixed in with the liquid. If not, I need a second sample from the athlete.

The last step for Scott is to take the box to a UPS shipping center, where he sends off the package (labeled "biological substance")

to the USADA lab, and then he's done. He gets a receipt and heads off to his next test. Scott figures that he carries out about three tests a week on average, and gets paid about $100 to $150 a test.

It's okay money, but it's not a full-time job for me. Sometimes I'm actually late for my day job. Luckily I have an understanding boss. He even jokes around with me. He yells, "Out on another pee job?" at me if I come in late. But I love what I do.

One last little detail is worth mentioning. The samples don't have the athletes' names on them, so the lab is dealing only with numbers. The athlete is notified of the results, whether positive or negative. If the test is positive, then the athlete's name and the penalty are released via the USADA website.

I know I've tested athletes who have been using drugs, but I can't really know if it came from one of my tests or not. I'm immensely disappointed when I hear that an athlete has tested positive, but I also know I'm doing my bit to keep sports clean.

How does someone become a doping control officer? For Scott it started with a deep-seated sense of fairness …

Growing up, if my friends and I were playing sports or board games, I was the kid who wanted everyone to play by the rules. I hated cheaters.

… that took a weird turn in college.

A friend of mine from grad school was a doping control officer. One day he asked me to go along as a chaperone. I said, "Collect

someone's pee? You're kidding me. That's too weird!" Then he said it paid, and I said, "Where do I sign up?"

A few years after Scott graduated, he saw there was a job opening for a doping control officer in his area. He applied and was accepted. The next step was a week-long training session at USADA headquarters in Colorado.

Scott has to watch as the athlete provides his urine sample.

This mostly involved practice sessions to make sure I knew the right steps in the right order and could ensure that the lab would get clean samples and the athlete would feel comfortable. I'd been helping my friend for a while, so I passed the exams easily.

This opened up a new world for Scott. He was already a sports fan, but now he was meeting athletes from all sorts of different sports. Scott was testing rowers, judokas, runners, swimmers – anyone within two hundred miles of his house could show up on his list.

We try to make the testing process friendly and relaxed, so we talk about their sports and their training. I'm always blown away by how hard these people work, how crazy their lives can be, and how exciting. I tested one guy just after he'd returned from Europe and just before he was about to leave for the Olympics in China.

When people think of anti-doping workers they often envisage clean-sport crusaders who are out to get the bad guys. Scott says that's not really the case.

It may sound odd, but I feel like I'm part of their team. I'm not against them or out to get them. I'm in some way with them in their competitions. I know that most of these athletes are clean. I also feel sad for the other athletes who get tainted or victimized by the cheaters.

Scott has been able to avoid the cynicism that sometimes affects sports fans, the "all athletes are guilty until proven innocent" mentality that can creep in when positive tests dominate the sports news.

If anything, I have become more of a sports fan. I root for the good guys. Maybe it's just human nature that some people will always cheat. I'm more interested in validating the effort and hard work of the people who don't cheat. That's why I call the samples "liquid gold" – because they are helping to secure the sanctity of sport.

And every time he sends a UPS package of "liquid gold" to Colorado, Scott knows he's doing just that.

Chapter 16

THE CHICKEN THAT NEVER LAYS AN EGG

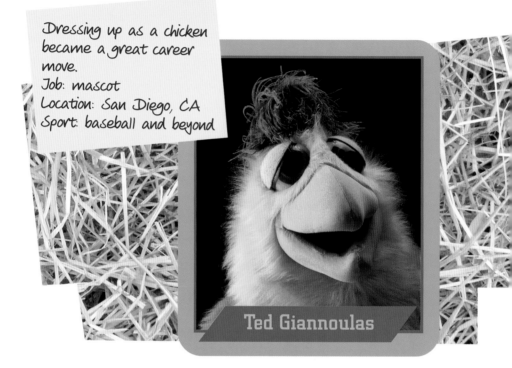

Dressing up as a chicken became a great career move.
Job: mascot
Location: San Diego, CA
Sport: baseball and beyond

Ted Giannoulas

These days almost every sports team has some mascot or other. There's the guy in the shark suit in San Jose. There are dancing gophers in Regina, parrots in Pittsburgh, and whatever the Phillie Phanatic is supposed to be in Philadelphia.

Mascots are everywhere now, but it's a recent phenomenon. In fact, all these strange creatures can trace their family trees back to a chicken – the Famous Chicken. The Chicken was born as a publicity stunt for a radio station in the early 1970s, and it created a completely new tradition. Well, actually, Ted Giannoulas did. He is the man inside the chicken suit.

When I was growing up I loved sports, but I don't remember any mascots at all on TV or at games. My high school had a cardinal costume, but it was basically a bird head that a cheerleader would put on in front of the crowd, run up and down the court, and then take off. That was it – not a lot of fun.

Ted didn't set out to change that situation by becoming the Famous Chicken. He wanted to be a journalist, but fate had a different plan. One day when Ted was sitting in a hallway at his college in San Diego, a representative from the local rock radio station came looking for cheap labor.

The Olympics have featured some of the stranger mascots in sports. Atlanta in 1996 had Izzy, short for "What is he?" No one was quite sure what the answer to that question was, but organizers sold a lot of souvenirs. In 2000 in Sydney there were three official mascots, but a local TV show trumped them all when it introduced its own unofficial mascot: "Fatso the Fat-Arsed Wombat." The anti-mascot became a huge hit with fans and Australian athletes, who posed with a stuffed version of Fatso. Today there's a Fatso statue outside the main stadium. The other mascots? Forgotten.

The station wasn't doing well in the ratings, so they were trying to come up with some ideas to get free publicity. I said I'd do anything and was hired on the spot, for two dollars an hour.

One of the crazier PR ideas was to have Ted dress up in a chicken costume with the call letters of the radio station on the front and go to public events. The first outfit was just a rented chicken suit, like one you might wear for Halloween. He started out by visiting San Diego's world-famous zoo, handing out Easter eggs. That worked pretty well, but Ted thought they could do even better.

I figured that a sporting event would be a good place to get some attention. It was also a sneaky way for me to get free admission to a baseball game. I was just trying to keep my foot in the door at the station so they would maybe give me some on-air work. It didn't work out quite the way I had planned.

Ted showed up in the suit at opening day in 1974, along with a high school friend. People stared at him, sure enough, but he knew he'd have to add some pizzazz to his routine to really get their attention. Since he couldn't remember any mascots from his childhood, he drew on other inspirations.

I love slapstick comedy, so I tried to act like the greats: Charlie Chaplin, the Three Stooges, the Marx Brothers. Steve Martin was starting to get big laughs around then, so I was also inspired by him. Instead of sitting there, I wandered around the stands trying to have fun with the people in the crowd.

Ted improvised. He heckled the opposing players with funny gestures. He and his friend got into mock arguments over the game. He stole his buddy's hot dog. He handed out free stuff from the radio station. It worked out so well, Ted came back for more games. His mother, a seamstress, also stitched him a much better-looking costume – more like a cartoon chicken and less like a big papier-mâché clown mask.

The New York Mets claim they began the mascot craze in the 1960s, with Mr. Met. But Mr. Met was really a papier-mâché baseball head they would put on the batboy for opening day. It was technically a mascot but not really much like the active – and comedy-based interactive – mascots we see today.

The chicken, and the age of the mascot, had arrived. The crowd loved it, and it wasn't just the huge laughs that provided the evidence. The San Diego Padres were far from a contending team, yet attendance went up. The radio station, which had been last in the ratings, jumped to the top.

Soon the Padres invited me to do stuff on the field as well. I decided to "cavort" as much as possible. I started acting as if I were coaching first base. A mascot and on the field? That

was unheard of, completely unprecedented. I would argue with the umpires – that would get a huge roar.

Ted starting adding all sorts of slapstick bits to his routine. He would give chicken suits to a bunch of younger fans and have them follow him onto the field, like a family crossing the road. He would get opposing players to pretend they were fighting with him.

I love it when there's physical humor, especially when the visiting team plays along. There's a neat bit where they chase me and then the whole team jumps on me in a big dog-pile. It's fun, and the fans always ask for that one when I perform at a game.

Before, the field had always been seen as sacred ground, but the Chicken opened it up to the fans – at least in their imagination. And he wasn't just improvising the role of a mascot; he was changing the whole fan experience.

I also introduced recorded music to the sports stadiums. Most places had only organs or some type of live music. I wanted to do my routines to modern rock, so I would bring along a boom box and they would hold it up to the microphone. Now every stadium plays rock and roll.

Pretty soon the Chicken was getting all kinds of different gigs. He was asked to show up at street festivals, political rallies, and concerts. He once made Elvis Presley laugh so hard that he had to stop singing mid-song. Ted had found his career, and it wasn't journalism.

It hasn't always been a smooth ride. In the late 1970s, Ted and his original employer, the radio station, split. The station managers weren't happy with Ted's desire to do more and more public events. Was the Chicken getting bigger than the station? The station fired Ted and tried to prevent him from appearing in the suit.

The case went all the way to the California Supreme Court. I won. I was a free agent and could work for anyone I pleased. I even redesigned the suit, along with my mother, to show that it was a rebirth for me and the Chicken.

The new suit was unveiled during yet another moment of on-field theater. A police motorcade escorted a giant Styrofoam egg into the San Diego ballpark. The players lowered the egg onto the field as the theme from the movie *2001: A Space Odyssey* played in the background, and Ted "hatched" in his revamped suit.

The appearance requests kept rolling in. Other sports teams asked him to be part of their entertainment package as well.

You have to tailor your act to the different sports. There's lots of down time in baseball, so if you do a comedy sketch the fans can watch you without taking away from the game. But in hockey or basketball there's stuff happening all the time. You have to be creative. Luckily I grew up playing hockey, so I can skate well enough to do bits on the ice between periods.

Everything can be a prop. Basketball hoops can be used for crazy dunks, and football uprights can be used to kick stuff through. The glass that surrounds a

> Hockey has a particular attraction for Ted. He grew up in London, Ontario, and was a goalie for years. He says wearing all that heavy equipment was good training for wearing a chicken suit.

hockey rink can be an impromptu canvas of sorts. Ted particularly likes rinks where he can get into the seats next to the penalty box.

I'll bring along a crayon and write "I'm with Stupid" on the glass. It takes a while for the players in the box to catch on. Then they play along and laugh.

But no matter where he performs, Ted says he makes sure that he is only part of the experience, never more important than the game. He got angry when he saw the Calgary Flames mascot, Harvey the Hound, bait opposing players during a game. Harvey actually leaned over the glass into the Edmonton Oilers' bench area. Oilers coach Craig MacTavish eventually yanked out the mascot's tongue.

That was a no-no. You have to respect the game. When I do a bit with an opposing player, it's away from the action. They are gracious to me and will play along because they know that I won't upstage the sport.

Ted was a young man when he first started doing his physical

comedy. Years later, he's still the man in the chicken suit, and he doesn't see himself stopping anytime soon. He's certainly still popular, appearing at more than 250 events a year.

It's not easy to do physical humor, even without a chicken suit on, so imagine doing all those stunts while wearing thick, heavy fabric.

The Chicken has appeared in TV shows, ads, and movies – he was one of the stars of the cult hit *Attack of the Killer Tomatoes*. He was also the official mascot for the first T-ball game at the White House, back in 2001.

I've been injured, but I've never missed a game in my career. I have to stay in good shape for sure, just like an athlete. And I always bring a few suits to each game. They can get pretty sweaty, so I have to change frequently during games. And if it's raining the suits can get really heavy.

Ted's mother made all his suits for years. She died a few years ago, but Ted proudly points out that one of her original Famous Chicken suits hangs in the Baseball Hall of Fame in Cooperstown, New York. His costumes are now made to order by a clothing company in California.

Fame has followed him all through his career. *Sporting News* magazine named him one of the hundred most powerful people in sports of the twentieth century. Who else was on the list? Only Babe Ruth, Wayne Gretzky, Muhammad Ali, and Ted Turner. All that could go to a person's head, chicken or human. But Ted says he tries not to take himself too seriously.

Family helps.

We'll be watching sports on TV and yet another mascot will show up, and my wife will turn to me and say, "There, I hope you're satisfied."

And knowing his role helps.

I am proud to say that I am like the court jester in the Middle Ages – "loved by the commoners and the king." I've met a lot of famous people, but really the greatest moment for me happens every time I do a routine and hear fifty thousand fans laughing. They are having a good time. There's nothing as beautiful as the sound of laughter.

Chapter 17

THE HORSE MAN

He's done everything from sitting in the saddle to shoveling the stables.
Job: trainer
Location: Toronto, ON
Sport: horse racing

Ian Black

Thundering hooves flash in the sunlight as the front pack of horses makes the final turn and heads into the home stretch. The leaders are crammed close together, hugging the white wooden rail at Woodbine Racetrack, leaning into the curve. Chunks of turf fly into the air as the horses furiously attempt to pull ahead. Even the fans in the stands can hear their deep, heavy breaths as the horses struggle for air. It looks like it's going to be a photo finish!

Ian Black is standing as close to the track as he can get. His horse, Mike Fox, is battling for the finish line. Right now Mike is in third place, but just a few strides behind the leader. Jockey Emma-Jayne Wilson is handling him perfectly. Ian can hear the jockeys yelling to their horses, encouraging them with words and an occasional crack of the whip. This is one of the oldest and biggest horse races in the world: the Queen's Plate.

Many horse races are run on dirt tracks or turf. Some, including the races at Woodbine, are run on a surface called Polytrack, which was designed by a former equestrian named Martin Collins. He came up with a mixture of sand, carpet fibers, and recycled rubber. It's soft, which is good for the horses and the jockeys if they get thrown. It also handles weird weather that can turn turf or dirt into a muddy mess.

If Emma-Jayne and Mike can cross the finish line first, they will win a million-dollar prize. Ian knows what it's like to be in the thick of the battle. He used to be a jockey.

How can I describe what it's like to be on a thoroughbred? It's like being in a really nice sports car – it's fast, it's smooth. Of course, I've also been on horses that felt like old clunkers or bikes with flat tires. They take more work.

His jockey days are long gone, so all Ian can do is watch how well Emma-Jayne is handling the job. Ian is now a trainer, and Mike Fox is definitely the kind of racehorse that feels like a sports car. As the trainer, Ian is like the head coach of the team that has brought Mike so close to victory.

I tell people that the trainer does about 20 percent of the total job. The horse does most of the work, of course. Then there's the jockey, the grooms, the exercise riders. I just oversee it all.

The Queen's Plate is the oldest thoroughbred race in North America. It was first run in 1860, and Queen Victoria donated a trophy to the winner worth fifty guineas (about $3400 in today's money). Thoroughbreds are a particular breed of horse, but the term can sometimes refer to any purebred horse. And the Queen's Plate is not actually a plate these days but a gold cup.

Ian is being a bit humble with the 20 percent estimate. He also helps figure out the strategy for each race. It's based on his observations of the track conditions and his knowledge of the horse.

Ian and jockey Emma-Jayne Wilson.

Some horses respond well when they start fast, so the jockey and I make sure that happens. Others need to be held back and then encouraged near the end of the race to catch up. But once the race starts, anything can happen, and then the jockey and the horse need to adjust.

Ian has been a trainer for only a short time, and this is one of his first big races. He says it's a different challenge for him and admits there are question marks about how successful he will be in this new role. Of course, it's not all new to him – Ian has done just about every other imaginable job in horse racing.

There are successful trainers out there who have never raced, but I think it gives me an advantage. I know how to communicate with jockeys and managers. Being a trainer means you're in charge of the team, but I know what all the team members have to do.

Ian doesn't own the horses, but he watches over every part of their lives. He says most of his work is done before the race starts. Part of that happens years before, when he first examines the young foals. It's his trained eye that figures out which horses will become racers and which horses won't. Part of that ability comes from a lifetime of experience.

I grew up on a farm in England, and we rode horses all the time. I left home at sixteen to become a jockey, then worked as a farm manager after moving to North America. I've been around them all my life.

Ian knows that his ability to pick winners also comes from all the hard work he puts in at the farm. It can take months to find out what kind of horse he is dealing with.

First the horse has to be "broken." That means getting it used to wearing a saddle, having the weight of a rider on its back. They can buck and snort and bolt just like in a rodeo, so you have to be careful. And you have to be patient – it can take six weeks to get a horse ready to safely carry a rider.

Once the horse is broken, it's time to see what kind of racer it could be. Ian sets up a plan of different distances for the horse to run, in all sorts of conditions: muddy, rain, dry grass, wet grass. He looks for what he calls the "action" of the horse – how it strides and how it handles the physical demands of the pounding on its body. But he's also looking for something else.

Attitude is so important. People don't always realize that. Is the horse happy doing this hard work? Does it exert itself or quit when

the pace and distance increase? An unhappy horse or a lazy horse is never going to win, no matter how beautiful, strong, or well trained. Natural talent is only part of the story.

Ian says horses are like people. They want attention; they want to impress others and be loved. It's easy to love Mike Fox, especially now, as he's catching up to the lead horse in the pack. Ian smiles, remembering the first time he saw Mike take a turn on a track.

He's a special horse. He was big, strong, and muscular, so he looked great. Above all else, he trained well. Mike loves being pushed to go faster. He enjoys racing, and that makes it a joy to train and then to watch him.

Ian watches his horses closely during both training and races, and not just to admire their power and beauty. Injuries are common and can fell even the best horses. Sometimes a change in attitude can signal that the horse isn't feeling well or has a hidden injury.

Horses can't talk, so you have to look for symptoms of trouble in other ways. Every morning we check the horses over completely. We place our hands on their legs and bodies and feel for heat – heat can signal an injury or an infection. But I can also tell that if a horse is behaving strangely, something else might be happening.

Sometimes when a horse seems unwell, there's something really bad going on. Ian has had to put down injured horses. "It breaks your heart," he says.

The problems aren't always physical. Stress can be a big concern, particularly when a race is far away and the horse has to travel. High-stakes racing is a worldwide phenomenon, and Ian often sends horses to Japan or Dubai.

Horses under stress don't eat. That's a big sign that people don't always look for. A horse has to travel by plane for as long as twenty hours to get to a race. There's always someone with him, but that's a long time to be cooped up in a box.

Luckily for both Ian and Mike Fox, today's race is at Woodbine, only a short drive from the farm – no plane trips for either of them today. Mike stables at the track during racing season, but Ian spends each morning at the farm with his thirty or so other horses.

They are like my children. I love them all, and each has different abilities.

Ian spends as much time as he can with the horses, building up a relationship with each one. Some are just being broken, while others are about to start racing. All, he jokes, are also adept at eating – and pooping.

I need to change my clothes a lot. I don't notice the smell when I'm at the stable, but then I'll walk inside for lunch and everyone will smell me coming a mile away!

Big races happen worldwide, and travel can be very tough for any animal. Horses stand the whole time, so they need to be well supported. You may have seen them traveling in the back of a truck, with a special harness on in case they get bumped around. It's much the same on a plane. The truck compartment they travel in is lifted onto the plane with a forklift. Most horses want to face the way the plane is heading, just as most people do. Attendants are with the horses the whole time in case they need food, medical attention, or just a calm, soothing voice.

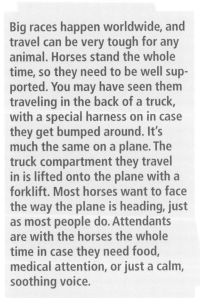

Ian is in his best clothes today because he's hoping to be in photos at the winner's circle. And that's starting to look like a distinct possibility. Mike Fox looks relaxed as he catches up to the front horse. The finish line is just yards away, but Ian is confident that Mike will pull into the lead. It's a turf track in good shape, and Ian knows this is exactly the type of racing that Mike loves.

Mike wasn't the pre-race favorite and he was four lengths back early in the race, but I knew he could come back. Emma-Jayne is a big part of that as well.

Lots of people in the stands behind Ian are cheering as well – at least, the ones who have placed bets on Mike Fox. Gambling is a big part of the business side of horse racing. Today's $600,000 first prize, or purse, comes from the ticket windows where race fans place their bets.

I get people coming up to me all the time asking me if my horse is going to win, or if my horse is in top shape. They are looking for inside information before they place their bets. I always tell them that I'm confident my horse will run well, but that there are many variables once the starting gates open.

Ian accepts that wagering is a big part of the thrill of race day for the fans, but he stays out of it himself.

I just worry about getting the horses in the best condition for the race. I figure that if my horse wins, everybody will be happy. Some people get a kick out of wagering, and they pay for the prizes through the bets they place, but it's not for me.

Emma-Jayne Wilson (#9) rides Mike Fox to victory.

Now just a few strides are left in the race. The thunder of hooves is being drowned out by the cheers of the crowd. The race is coming down to the very end. Just before the wire, Mike Fox pulls ahead of the other horses. He crosses the finish line first!

Ian jumps up and down. What a race! What a win! The people who bet on Mike are also jumping up and down – they've hit a big payday.

Ian rushes down to the winner's circle. Emma-Jayne and Mike are already there, covered by a purple and gold blanket made of flowers. Ian gives Mike Fox a big kiss and

Emma-Jayne Wilson is the first female jockey to win the Queen's Plate. She had always loved horses, and when she was twenty she wrote a note to herself promising to become a successful jockey. She found the note tucked in a book the night before the Queen's Plate. She has gone on to race internationally in Hong Kong, Dubai, and, of course, near her home at Woodbine.

Emma-Jayne a giant hug. All of them get big smiles from Mike's owner, D. Morgan Firestone.

Then they all pose for pictures with the flowers and then the trophy. This is a sweet moment for everyone involved in the team. Mike Fox has had his first big win. It's Emma-Jayne's first Queen's Plate win. Ian has spent a lifetime in the sport but barely two years as a trainer, and here he is at the top of his sport.

Ever since I left home I've been able to work with horses. I know how lucky I am.

Chapter 18

ON THE HOT SEAT

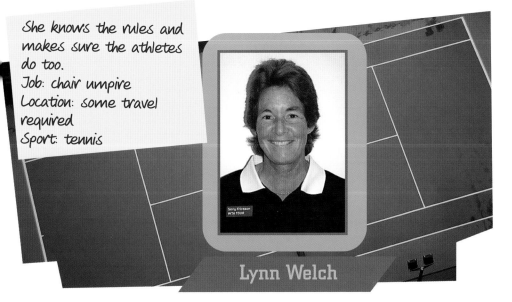

She knows the rules and makes sure the athletes do too.
Job: chair umpire
Location: some travel required
Sport: tennis

Lynn Welch

Lynn Welch remembers her training very clearly. How could she not? It's still ringing in her ears – literally. One of her instructors was assigned to scream abuse at her, swear at her, and argue a line call as vociferously as possible. Lynn was okay with that, despite the piercing volume. It was part of her professional training to become a tennis chair umpire.

I had been an amateur player, a teaching pro, and a line umpire. Then I was asked if I would like to be a chair umpire. I don't like confrontation, but part of my training involved getting yelled at. It's one of the drills the instructors do to see if you're ready for the pressure and possible arguments that arise during big matches.

As a tennis chair umpire, Lynn sits on a tall chair that's set up right at the net, in the exact middle of the action. In a match with no electronic line calling (Hawk-Eye system), she has the final say on whether a ball is in or out, and she is the first authority on whether a rule has been broken. (The referee is the final authority on all questions of tennis law, and the referee's decision is final.) If the players are unhappy, they don't have far to go to complain, and they let Lynn know what they think.

US tennis superstar John McEnroe changed what was considered "appropriate" on-court behavior. He was both immensely talented and immensely obnoxious. McEnroe would argue calls with umpires, swear at them, yell at them, and even smash his racket against the ground. Sometimes umpires would penalize him for his unsportsmanlike conduct, but the fans ate it up, often either cheering or booing his antics.

Tennis players get caught up in the heat of the moment. I know that. Sometimes the best thing to do is just not say anything and let them vent their anger. You have to maintain a calm façade.

That can be easier said than done. The players are pumped up by the competition and the rush of physical effort, and things can escalate quickly. Have you ever found yourself in an argument where you know you'll regret what you're saying but say it anyway because you're so angry?

My job is not to get angry or officious but to get the match going again. I listen and, when necessary, respond. Some things that I've said in response to a question haven't always completely satisfied the player. When they finish yelling and turn back to play, I've learned to let them have the last word or else the whole flare-up could start again.

Lynn has had to develop a thick skin over the years.

You can't take it personally. You also can't back down just because they are unhappy. If a player has served a ball that is outside the

service box, for example, I have to make the call if my line umpire has not. It doesn't matter how much the player may disagree; you have to make the overrule if you see a clear mistake. You must also enforce the rules. And it doesn't matter whether it's the first point of the match or the match point. You are there to make sure the game is fair for everyone.

Technology has helped settle many disputes about whether a ball was in or not. The Hawk-Eye system uses cameras and computer imaging to determine exactly where the ball hit the playing surface. On close points, the players can challenge the original call and ask the chair umpire to refer to the system.

That's taken a lot of pressure off the umpires and other officials. But it's only part of the job.

Sometimes Lynn has to keep track of more than just the fuzzy yellow tennis balls and where they land. She also needs to have a deep knowledge of the complex rules of tennis. These determine such things as when the players switch sides on the tennis court and when they can talk to their coaches, for example. Only Women's Tennis Association tournaments and Fed Cup and Davis Cup ties actually allow on-court coaching.

At the 2009 US Open, Serena Williams ended a match thanks to her reaction to a foot-fault call. The lineswoman saw that Williams had stepped on the baseline while serving a second serve and called a foot-fault. Williams began yelling, swearing, and saying things that threatened the official. The referee was called to court by the chair umpire, and the decision was made to issue Serena with a code violation point penalty for unsportsmanlike conduct (she had already received a code violation warning for racket abuse earlier in the match). The foot-fault call on the second serve meant that Serena lost that point, which now set up match point for her opponent, Kim Clijsters. The code violation point penalty ended the match and Clijsters won. Lynn wasn't the umpire that day, but she understood and agreed with the ump's decision. Rules are rules.

Lynn also knows the rules about how long players can take between points, and how much time they are allowed for medical time-outs (MTOs) and changeover treatments when they're injured. If players take too long to recover and get back to play after an MTO, Lynn can penalize them using the code for delay of game. She starts with a warning, then a point, then whole games, if necessary. Depending on the timing, that could end up being the deciding point or game of a match.

I was working a really long and intense match in Doha [in Qatar], and Caroline Wozniacki started having really bad muscle cramps. She was down on the ground. As a human being, part of me wanted to go to her and help. But as chair umpire I knew I couldn't. She had already received her one and only three-minute medical time-out allowed for cramping. She now had to get up and play within twenty seconds or I was going to have to penalize her with a code violation for delay of game. It was a really close match, so every point was important. Wozniacki ended up going over the twenty seconds and I had to issue her a code violation warning for delay of game. After this she got up and played in time before I had to give her a code violation point penalty. If she had not gotten up in time, the code would have continued to be applied, with the point penalty followed by game penalties. A match could end like that, or the player might not be able to continue and just retire.

It's not just injuries that worry Lynn. Sometimes it's about when a player can go to the bathroom. If you Google Lynn's name, one of the first stories that comes up is about when she would not allow Maria Sharapova to take a pee break during a match in 2008!

It's all about fair play. Sometimes a player will make excuses or

Lynn is sometimes asked to confirm where a ball has landed.

requests to leave the court for a toilet break, for example, in order to slow down the play of a match that's not going well. It is up to me to make sure that these requests come at an appropriate time, and there are guidelines in place for this. Toilet breaks are to be taken at a set break or before the player's own serve. If the player chooses to go before their opponent's serve, they are on their own

time. That means they have to get back quickly or face time viola-
tions. I start with a warning and then issue a point penalty for
each subsequent infraction until the player returns to court and is
ready to play.

The best matches, Lynn says, are the ones where the crowd or
TV audience doesn't even realize she's there. That means the players are happy and the crowd is caught up in the action, not
distracted by courtside antics or arguments. The calm also allows
her to enjoy one of the great perks of her job – being really close to
a game she loves.

There is unbelievable noise when you get that close to the action.
Some of the best players, such as the Williams sisters, hit the ball
with such force that there is a loud pop as the ball hits the racket
strings, and there are loud grunts as they expel air with the effort
of every stroke.

Lynn played the game at a high level and continues to teach
tennis when not on tour, so she knows how elusive things such as
that *pop* can be. She admits there's a temptation to get caught up in
the drama, the excitement of the play, but if she focuses her mind
on her job she can enjoy the whole experience.

I am able to watch a great player such as Roger Federer with dif-
ferent eyes. The umpire in me is watching to make sure the ball is
in and that there are no violations. My inner coach and player are
amazed at how he keeps his head absolutely still as he makes con-
tact with the ball. And the speed of the game at that level is
unbelievable. I'm very lucky to be able to see this up close and to
have the best seat in the house.

It's an amazingly public life for someone from a small town in Maine who says she would really prefer to stay out of the spotlight. She loved being a line umpire because she was close to the action but was able to stay mostly anonymous. But when she was asked to be a chair umpire, she rose to the challenge. She is very good at her job, so there she is on camera at the world's biggest tournaments, standing between the greatest players in the world and their thousands of fans.

I remember the first time I was an umpire at the US Open in New York. Arthur Ashe Stadium is huge. I asked a colleague of mine if she had any tips for dealing with the pressure. She said, "Don't look up." I didn't know what she meant. Then I walked onto the court and looked up – and up and up and up. There was a sea of people rising up to the sky, it seemed. And was it ever loud!

The anticipation of umpiring a game still sometimes fills her stomach with butterflies, like an actor going on stage. Lynn says

that "edge" of nerves helps her realize, every time she sits in the umpire's chair, how great her job is.

Lynn has presided over matches from small towns all the way up to the four Grand Slams (the Australian Open, the French Open, Wimbledon, and the US Open) and the Olympics (Atlanta in 1996, Sydney in 2000, and Greece in 2004), and everywhere in between. She tries to arrive a few days before an overseas tournament. It helps her to adjust to the new time zone and relax a bit before the start of play.

I love history and exploration. I was invited to a tournament in Luxembourg, and I just walked and walked around the city looking at the amazing architecture. In China I made sure to take time to visit the Great Wall and the Forbidden City. I am also lucky to have a job that lets me see the world, and I feel a responsibility to take advantage of that.

Each tournament and venue is different and often presents different challenges. Sometimes it's the court. The French Open is played on clay, which makes for a slower game. Wimbledon is played on grass, which is very fast. The US Open is on a hard surface called DecoTurf, which is moderately fast. The elements can also be a huge challenge. In Australia it's the heat.

I have never experienced heat like the heat they get in Australia. I remember opening the door of the umpire's room and it was like walking into an oven. Sometimes it gets close to 40 degrees Celsius [104 degrees Fahrenheit], and that's not safe for anybody, so we have had to suspend match play until the temperature dropped.

In other places, such as the outdoor US Open, it's rain.

One year it rained so much we were constantly starting and stopping and then restarting matches again. It took us four days to complete one match. It's tough to stay focused and alert for four days as you go on and off the court for numerous rain delays. Some umpires do sudoku on breaks, read books, or solve crosswords. I watched a lot of raindrops fall and did a lot of reading.

What's her favorite place? Not surprisingly, it's a venue that embraces both history and her favorite sport.

Wimbledon. It has such history and tradition. The royal box is on my right as I sit in the umpire's chair on center court. Tennis has been played there for more than a hundred years. And it's played on grass that is just beautiful. It's quite special.

Chapter 19

IN THE BLINK OF A LENS

Can you ski downhill backward carrying a heavy
camera? Brian can.
Job: cameraman
Location: Calgary, AB
Sport: everything from
badminton to bobsleigh

Brian Burnett

It's Lake Louise, Alberta, in December and it's freezing. Freezing freezing – 30 degrees below zero freezing. Brian Burnett should be inside in front of a warm fire or drinking a hot cup of tea. Instead he's on the side of a mountain, hopping from treetop to treetop, stringing thousands of feet of video cable.

In a few hours the top skiers in the world are going to be flying down this mountainside. Brian is one of the best camera operators in the sports business, and he is making sure the race gets broadcast around the world.

We use the cable to carry the images from several cameras down to the broadcast truck. The hard thing is that you can't let the cables get buried under the snow, because they'll freeze underneath and then you'll never get them out.

The cold is going to get even worse. Once Brian has finished running the cables, he'll step behind one of the cameras. The cameras on the side of the course are as close to the skiers as possible, and exposed to the elements. In order to get the best shots, Brian will be outside for hours, trying to stand as still as possible – not easy to do when you're shivering.

Skiing is different because you capture only a small part of the race, maybe the three seconds from when the skier crests the hill to where he or she disappears from view. But you have to be ready for anything. They almost all follow the same line down the hill, but you need to be ready to catch the one who takes a different line or maybe veers off course and crashes.

There's one more thing you should know. No matter how cold it gets, Brian wears only thin cloth gloves, with no extra padding or insulation.

Zooming in is an art. You have to feel how the camera is moving and focusing. You can't have big, thick gloves or you'll lose that feel. So you do your best to catch each skier as she or he flies down the hill, then you slip your hands into your coat pockets and warm them with heated gel-packs.

THE BLINK OF AN EYE
One of the most famous shots in the history of skiing lasts only a few seconds. Hermann Maier was training at the 1998 Nagano Olympics when his ski got caught in a rut. He flew through the air and crashed through fence after fence after fence. Just a few days later he won a gold medal, earning the nickname "the Herminator." If the camera operator hadn't been alert, he could easily have missed the shot. Instead it helped make Maier a legend in the sport.

Brian's days can start before dawn and end long after dark. The days can be even longer if cold weather freezes the camera bays or if there's a glitch in the wiring or other transmission systems.

If the system isn't working, the race doesn't make it to TV. So you work until the problems are fixed – no matter how long that takes.

Brian isn't always working the sideline cameras. He often operates the camera at the starting gate, inside a large hut at the very top of the mountain. It's more sheltered than the cameras course-side, thus slightly warmer, but the position poses different challenges. Brian films the skiers as they go through the gate and head down the mountainside, but he's also responsible for "tracking shots" – pictures of the skiers as they warm up or wait their turn.

You have to know who all the top skiers are, for every team. Sometimes the director will say, "I need a shot of Bode Miller." I have to find him in the crowd of people in the starting hut, and I have to get the shot fast. If you're a rookie camera operator, all the skiers look the same – they all have helmets and racing suits. But I can tell in an instant who's who.

Skiing has a place very close to Brian's heart. It's one of his favorite sports to participate in and one of his favorites to cover. He lives full-time in Calgary, Alberta, close to one of the best ski venues in the world: Lake Louise. He's followed many of the top skiers since they were competing at the junior level.

I was covering a big race before the 2010 Olympics. John Kucera was one of the medal hopefuls for Canada, but he crashed into the netting and busted his leg. Even though I'm not officially part of the team, I was heartbroken. You still have to do your job and capture the drama on camera, but you hurt inside.

Brian has filmed a number of profiles as well as events (at least

one co-worker says he's famous as "the guy who can ski backward holding a camera"). As a result he's been able to visit the homes of many of the best athletes in the world.

You get to know them as people. It can make it hard to watch them get injured, but it also makes it mean even more when they win. It's like watching a neighbor or a friend do something great.

Brian has worked many Olympic Games including in 2008, in Beijing.

Another advantage to living in Calgary is that Brian gets to cover almost any sport you can imagine. Calgary hosted the Winter Olympic Games in 1988 and it still hosts numerous World Cup events in every winter sport. The city is also the main training center for the Canadian Olympic team and home to professional hockey and football teams. So Brian has filmed top-level competition in everything from badminton to bobsleigh.

Your job is essentially the same in each sport – you have to follow the action. But each sport presents different challenges too. In skiing you cover a small portion of the hill. You follow the skier for about three seconds and then turn the camera back to the top of the hill. In hockey you have to anticipate where the shot is going to come from and where the puck will go. Sometimes the best shots are away from the action.

Clearly experience is important, and Brian has plenty. He got his first gig way back in 1982. The technology has changed a lot since then.

My first handheld camera was a big, heavy thing. You had to hand-crank to zoom the lens for the close-ups. Now that's all automatic. There's a zoom capacity in the new camera that makes a smooth transition with the lens, not the clunk-clunk of the old cameras. It makes it way easier to get the shot right. And now there's HD [high-definition] *technology that has completely changed the way people experience the game.*

High definition (HD) has meant a revolution for everyone. For viewers, it means that the picture on the screen is almost as clear and detailed as real life. For camera operators such as Brian, it puts even more pressure on them to do a good job. Take a touchdown in football, for example. The instant replay isn't just for the viewers anymore; it's used by the officials too.

So you need to make sure that you don't just follow the ball from the quarterback through the air and into the receiver's hands. That's a beautiful shot, but you also have to make sure that you get the receiver's feet in the frame too. Was he out of bounds when he

caught the ball? With HD you can zoom right in to that tight shot of the toe and the lines on the field. Your shot could decide the winner of the Grey Cup.

HD technology has also helped Brian understand the sports themselves even better, especially when everything is slowed down.

It breaks down what's happening into milliseconds because you can see the action frame by frame. For example, I always knew good golfers were powerful. But with slow-motion replay with the detail of HD technology, you can actually see the way a rock-hard golf ball compresses like a soft sponge when it's hit with a driver. This allows a view of a whole different world!

Technology helped officials make a call that helped the New Orleans Saints win the Super Bowl in 2010. Saints receiver Lance Moore caught the ball on a two-point conversion and then dropped it. At least, that's how it appeared to the official on the field and the naked eye of the viewer. But the play was reviewed, and you could see on the detailed replay that Moore had caught the ball, controlled it, and crossed the goal line, then had the ball kicked loose. The officials overturned their original ruling and the play counted.

It's not just the detail of the picture but also the technology of the lenses themselves that blows him away. With the old lenses he could zoom to maybe forty times what you see with the naked eye. Now he can zoom up to a hundred times.

Let me put that in perspective. When I started, I could get a close-up of a player from the waist up. With a 100:1 ratio, I can zoom right in on the eyes. That doesn't just give you a better picture – it takes you right inside the emotion of the game. You can see what a player is thinking, feeling. Wow.

Brian at his perch catching the action at an NHL game in Calgary.

Not everything comes down to training and technology. Brian says that research is also a huge part of being prepared. He sits down before each game and reads the sports pages and searches the Internet for the big stories. That allows him to capture not just the action but the drama as well.

If I know the Flames' Cory Sarich has been injured for two weeks and then I see him show up for the pre-game warm-ups, I make sure to follow him with my camera. Is he skating well enough to play? Is he just trying out his legs to see if he's still hurt? If I don't get that on film, the audience at home won't get the whole story of the game.

It's a team effort to tell that story. Brian knows that his own shots will be part of a larger tapestry from a number of other camera operators. All the images are sent to the broadcast truck, where the director picks which pictures to put into the broadcast.

I am part of a team, and we all follow different parts of the action. It's all assembled by the director in the end, but I also know I need to be ahead of the director. If I wait to hear him tell me he wants a certain shot, I'll miss it. The games go too fast to wait. I have to anticipate what shot he'll be asking for so that I know it will be there when he wants it.

Brian calls his approach "aggressive camerawork." It's about being prepared and looking for the key shot – the shot that tells the real story of the race or the game. Maybe it's a shot of the winning score; maybe it's of a player who's made a big mistake and is looking crestfallen.

You have to focus, get yourself in a zone where your eyes are completely locked on to the action and your mind is focused on all the possible things that can go wrong or right. You don't know when you'll get that shot. You have to be prepared mentally and physically for your reaction time

The broadcast truck is a kind of a central hub for what gets to your TV. Most broadcasters have control rooms in their buildings, but if an event is outside (such as skiing), then the truck heads to the site as a mobile command center. From the outside it looks like an RV. Inside, it's an electronics lover's dream. One wall is lined with several TV screens, each showing the images being sent from specific cameras. There are mixing boards, sound systems, computers for placing graphics over the pictures, and often satellite dishes on top of the truck. The director calls which shots go to air live and also which shots need to be lined up for replays. Technicians are pushing buttons and adjusting knobs to make those directions a reality. During a big event it can seem like chaos to an outsider, with all the yelling and coded language (cameras are often referred to by number, so you might hear "Ready five, take five"), but to the people in the know, it's crazy coordination.

to be bang-on. You can't waver or get distracted. Only one shot is shown live, but all the shots are important.

Think about this the next time you see a TV broadcast crew analyze a big play. They use a variety of different shots from different angles, sometimes with close-ups and sometimes with wide-screen views of the whole playing surface. Some are shown in slow motion. Once pieced together, they tell the complete story of what happened. As Brian says, a good crew works like a well-tuned engine.

Like many camera operators, Brian's journey behind the camera started with a desire to be in front of it.

Every sports fan faces a time when they have to make a decision. I was pretty good at skiing and hockey, but I knew I wasn't going to become a professional. So I decided to go to school, to get an education. My mom asked me, "But what kind of education?" I didn't know.

One day Brian was sitting in his living room looking through piles of course books for universities, searching for inspiration on what to do with his life. The TV was on, airing a game on CBC-TV's *Hockey Night in Canada*.

And it hit me. The only reason I was able to watch the game was because someone was there to capture it on camera. I had always loved photography. I told myself right then and there that I was going to be a camera operator on Hockey Night in Canada.

Brian enrolled in the local institute of technology and studied broadcasting for two years. He did so well that he was hired right out of school by a local station. He rose up through the ranks, gaining

experience and accolades. A few years later he found himself right where he had planned – behind the camera at a *Hockey Night in Canada* game.

Brian covering the Edmonton-Carolina Stanley Cup Final in 2006.

I heard the theme music from the show on my headset as I got ready for the game to start. I can still feel the chill in my spine that I felt at that moment. I wasn't nervous; I was happy. I told myself, "Let's go! Bring it on!" I was like a kid. I even called home after the game to ask my mom and dad if they'd watched the game!

Brian has gone on to shoot many more hockey games. He's been to numerous Olympics, World Cup races, major championships in every sport. And he says he always has that same tingle of anticipation and joy when the race begins or the puck is dropped and his job is to capture it through the lens of his camera. He echoes the thought of almost everyone involved in *Game Day*: "I have the greatest job in the world."

Chapter 20

MUSIC AND MOVEMENT

A chance encounter with ribbons led to a lifelong love of skating.
Job: choreographer
Location: Los Angeles, CA
Sport: figure skating

Sarah Kawahara

Sarah Kawahara leans over the boards at her home skating rink in Los Angeles, California. She's watching the footwork of her latest figure skaters, the pairs team of Keauna McLaughlin and Rockne Brubaker, two-time national champions. Sarah is watching to make sure that their skates are rising and falling in rhythm with the music, and that they are enjoying the routine as well.

Sarah is the choreographer, the person who comes up with the programs that help athletes wow the judges.

Figure skating is a combination of entertainment and athleticism. In competition there are set rules about what kinds of elements have to be in a routine – certain lifts, jumps, and spins. At their technical core the routines are similar, so the choreography is really what sets one routine apart from another. It tells the story around the jumps and spins.

Today's competitive skating is very defined, with required elements. This change occurred in reaction to criticism that the sport's judges were being too subjective. So the rules were changed to establish a more exact scoring system for the jumps and spins.

In many ways the blueprint is more established today. But the choreographer adds the flair, the style. You're like the designer for a dress.

The first rehearsals are always shaky. The skaters are worrying about a hundred things: their timing, their position on the ice, how much speed they'll need to pull off the jumps and lifts, and the condition of the ice. Of course, there's also the pressure to do well and impress the judges. McLaughlin and Brubaker make up one of the top teams in the world. They trust that Sarah has made the right choices for them.

> Some jumps aren't allowed in figure skating, such as backflips and somersaults. Skaters will sometimes pull them out for exhibitions, but they'll lose points if they attempt them in competition.

The music has to match the skater. It's not just that you take a beautiful piece of music and give it to the skater and say, "This will be great." You have to know who they are as people and find a piece of music that will match the way they move, the way they feel. It has to let them express themselves. The skaters have to like the music; otherwise it's a dead end.

Sarah knows the importance of the beauty in skating. It all goes back to the moment she fell in love with the sport. She was six years

Classical music is the go-to music for figure skating for a number of reasons. It can be beautiful and lyrical, and it echoes the links between classical dance and figure skating. But there are practical reasons as well. The judges are usually much older than the performers, so they have different musical tastes. As well, only ice dancers are allowed to use music with lyrics, so most skaters find that orchestral pieces suit the speed and grace they are looking for. Younger skaters are starting to push the envelope a bit, but Sarah says you have to find a balance: "You can't make it too edgy or else the judges get turned off. So now many people choose movie themes, which are both modern and traditional."

old and her family had just moved to Toronto, where she grew up. She was on her way to ballet school when she passed an outdoor rink. A group of figure skaters was twirling around the ice.

They were all wearing ribbons and I thought it was the most beautiful thing. They were outdoors, skating so fast, with their ribbons fluttering in the breeze. I was six years old and I wanted to know how they got those ribbons. I didn't get ribbons in ballet school! I had never skated before, but I begged to be able to skate. That year for Christmas I got a pair of figure skates.

As soon as she laced on those skates, Sarah never wanted to take them off. Of course there were plenty of wobbles and spills along the way, but she knew from the start that she had found her passion.

I felt so comfortable in my body. I knew that I could move in different ways and that I could also be creative. I felt joy.

Dance remained a big part of her life. The conditioning, strength, balance, and grace she learned on the wooden floor of the ballet studio translated perfectly onto the ice.

Dance is wonderful – all about line, the connection of music and movement. When I was young, I loved to jump. In dance I rarely

got the chance to jump. But in figure skating you get to jump all the time. That was the clincher for me.

Sarah turned ten and was concentrating more and more on her skating. She competed at the national level but found that competition wasn't the best fit for her. She was more interested in exploring the limits of how you could tell a story on the ice and paint pictures through the medium of skating.

The Olympics were never really a goal for me. I had a great coach and choreographer named Osborne Colson, who would always ask me, "What are you trying to say through your skating?" He showed me that it wasn't just landing a jump that mattered but how you felt while doing it and how many ways you can express that same feeling. He'd suggest I look to the left while landing or turn a different way and do something unexpected. That became my journey and my calling, exploring the creative boundaries of the sport. He opened up my mind as a whole person, and that's what I try to do as well.

Osborne Colson was a legend in figure skating. He won two Canadian titles in the 1930s and went on to coach numerous champions, including Barbara Anne Scott, who won the Olympic title in 1948. He was also one of the first coaches for current Canadian champion Patrick Chan. He never slowed down, continuing to coach until his death in 2006.

When Sarah was seventeen, two things happened that would change her life. She was at the national championships. Her routine didn't score well with the judges, but a scout was there from the Ice Capades, the biggest touring show in the world. He was impressed by how

different Sarah was from the other skaters. She moved with athleticism but also with the grace of a ballerina, and she could combine her skating and her music in perfect harmony.

I was a nobody, but he saw something he liked. He offered me a job after the nationals and I joined them as part of the chorus skaters and as an understudy for a principal skater. Pretty soon I had impressed the producers of the show and was made a full principal skater.

This tied in with the second thing that happened at the nationals. Sarah watched the great skater Toller Cranston. According to the judges, he finished well behind the leaders, but he got standing ovations from the crowd. Cranston was well known as a perfectionist, a skater who had refused to sacrifice his artistic vision.

Toller was magnificent. Watching him skate and then get a standing ovation, when he had no chance of winning, was a highly charged visual moment for me.

Cranston was also one of the first skaters to realize the potential of taking his vision away from the rink and putting it on television. He had seen Sarah skate and knew she would be a perfect fit for his TV special *Strawberry Ice*. It mixed different musical numbers, everything from the conga to Broadway show tunes. He called her his muse – incredibly high praise.

He made a guest appearance with the Ice Capades and knew who I was. It turns out that he had seen me skate before as well. He told me that I was different because I was able to combine an artistic vision with the physical demands of the sport. I went on to help

Toller choreograph a Christmas TV special, The True Gift of
Christmas. *We are still friends.*

Sarah was awakening to the
seemingly limitless possibilities of
her sport. Soon she was approached
by other great skaters, such as
Peggy Fleming and Scott Hamilton,
to help them design routines. She
helped them develop traveling
shows that won critical and popular acclaim. Sarah began to skate
less often, spending more time
helping other skaters work on
their routines.

*Scott Hamilton was special as well.
He was a thinking skater, with a
great sense of humor. He was always
willing to take chances, and willing
to go through the struggle of looking
bad if he thought it would help him
improve and do something unique.
That takes confidence – in himself
and in me. He would trust me that a
routine that felt odd at first could be
great with hard work.*

Hamilton called Sarah "a genius."
They collaborated on a TV special
called *Scott Hamilton: Upside Down*.

Scott Hamilton (pictured above,
with Sarah) is one of the greatest
skaters of all time. He won
numerous US titles and world
championships, as well as the
Olympic gold medal in 1984. He
was smaller than most other
skaters (only five feet, two
inches), partly because of a child-
hood condition that delayed his
growth. But he made up for that
with unbelievable athleticism
and a physical style. After his
retirement from competition he
toured with numerous shows. He
also survived a battle with cancer
that briefly curtailed his professional career, but he came back
from that as well.

It was a rare luxury because I was involved in the whole process, from casting the skaters to the choreography and the camera angles. It was almost all male skaters, which is also rare. It gave me the chance to explore a more vigorous and quick style of choreography. There were lots of different tempos and very physical routines.

Sarah was the first skating choreographer to win an Emmy Award.

This was very different from the more graceful style she'd explored with Toller Cranston, and it allowed Sarah to grow and learn more. And the show was a ratings and critical hit. Sarah won an Emmy Award for outstanding choreography, the first skating choreographer ever to win that award.

That was totally unexpected. It's a strange thing to choreograph for TV, because you set your routines with the skaters to the music, but then the camera takes over and you view your choreography from one side. In order to see the movement from different sides

you have to move the camera or work with more than one camera. You have to trust everyone involved in the team – the producer, the director, and the camera operators. I think that this was possibly the best example of my work, certainly to that point in my career.

But it wasn't the last Emmy that she would win. Sarah had caught the eye of the producers of the 2002 Winter Olympic Games, which would be hosted by Salt Lake City, Utah. They had gone looking for a choreographer for the opening ceremonies, and they wanted someone based in the United States.

To work with Hamilton and other top American skaters, Sarah had moved to Los Angeles. She had also fallen in love and started a family, so a big event like that – close to home – was a perfect fit.

I love to keep my life diverse. That keeps it all interesting. But it was a big challenge. To begin with, the ceremonies took place outdoors in a giant football stadium, on a frozen ice surface that covered the whole field.

Sarah pulled out all the stops. She drew on every aspect of her career: dance, the visual arts, music. Skaters opened the ceremony carrying flags of all the Winter Olympics host cities. Then skaters emerged with "flames" flying behind them, their elaborate costumes portraying everything from "children of light" to cowboys. Some weren't on skates, but stilts.

They were local people who put up drywall. They stand on these five-foot-high stilts to help them finish the tall ceilings. So we had them dressed like magical snow creatures – the crones of the snowstorm. They walked on the ice stilts with skaters moving all around them.

She enlisted six hundred skaters of all skill levels and ages to take part.

I basically stripped the whole Salt Lake area of anyone who could skate forward and stop. If you could do that, you were in my show.

Many were figure skaters, some were speed skaters, and some were hockey players.

I loved my hockey players. I was asking them to do things that were really hard for them. There's a difference in the way they skate. Figure skaters are like big letter I's. They stand straight and shift their balance from one side to the other. Hockey players are like triangles. They lean forward when they skate, so you have to choreograph different movements for them.

Sarah even got her own children to lace up for the event; they lived close enough that her husband could drive them to and from rehearsals. The overriding challenge was that the ceremony needed to please both the crowd in the stadium and the millions watching on TV around the world.

It was so big and so complex. I looked at it like playing with building blocks. I worried about each block on its own, and then how they fit together into the big picture.

It was another hit, and Sarah won her second Emmy for outstanding choreography.

She had no plans to slow down. In 2007 she took on an even tougher challenge: choreographing the comedy movie *Blades of Glory*, with Will Ferrell and Jon Heder. The actors were not great

skaters, but they wanted to do as much of the action as they could (Heder actually broke an ankle trying one routine). And one of the cast members really impressed her.

Will Arnett is Canadian, he'd played hockey, and was willing to try figure skating. He even became quite a good pairs skater, skating with his real-life wife, Amy Poehler.

Sarah with world champion Kurt Browning.

Sarah has become the choreographer for *Oasis* and *Allure of the Seas*, the largest cruise ships in the world, which offer figure-skating shows as part of the entertainment. She has also choreographed shows at the Kennedy Center for the Arts in Washington, DC. She works with competitive skaters such as McLaughlin and Brubaker and Michelle Kwan, and she even helped the University of Miami's synchronized skating team win the US title. That's just a small part of Sarah's exhaustive list of achievements. Each one poses different challenges, but at the heart she feels they are all the same.

The sign of a successful choreographer is that they make the most out of what the individual skaters have. They all have different skill sets, different body types, different temperaments. So we need to know each other. I have always created best when I am engaged with the whole person I'm working with. Then we explore the creative sides of ourselves.

A young Sarah skating in the TV special STRAWBERRY ICE.

Sarah has an even easier way to sum up her approach to her career and the people she works with:

My job is to bring color into their lives.

THE FAN

You!

You are also a huge part of the success of game day. Maybe you are the lifelong fan who lives and dies with your team. Maybe you are the curious person who's decided to tag along with a friend to see what all the fuss is about at the arena or stadium. I hope this book helps you see that a team is more than just the athletes.

Maybe you're someone who would like to make it to the bigs some day, or maybe you realize you never will, but still love the game. Whatever your hopes and dreams the people in this book have had them too. What they all share is a passion for sports. They followed that passion, and it led them to rich, fulfilling lives.

Every person's story is different.

What's yours? And what will it be?

ACKNOWLEDGMENTS

There are many people to thank for this book. First of all Rick Wilks, who bought me a delicious coffee and suggested this great idea. Gillian Watts nursed it along. Sandra Booth and Sheryl Shapiro made it a visual success. Katie Hearn gave it some polish.

Phil Dugas, Glen Watson, Mark Crawley, Robin Brown, Teddy Katz, and everyone at CBC Radio made me think about sports critically—which made me smarter and more interested in always looking for the story behind the story.

I also have to thanks John Sliwa, a great family friend who got me hooked on sports, especially baseball, when I was just a young kid. He and his wonderful wife, Mary, also gave me their complete set of The Hardy Boys mysteries which got me just as hooked on reading and writing.

My family's help and support can't be calculated.

And of course, to all the amazing people who became the pages of this book and the many many more who make every game day happen.

IMAGE CREDITS

Annick Press Ltd.
All rights reserved. No part of this work covered by the copyrights hereon may be reproduced or used in any form or by any means – graphic, electronic, or mechanical – without the prior written permission of the publisher.

We acknowledge the support of the Canada Council for the Arts, the Ontario Arts Council, and the Government of Canada through the Canada Book Fund (CBF) for our publishing activities.

 ONTARIO ARTS COUNCIL
CONSEIL DES ARTS DE L'ONTARIO

Cataloging in Publication

Sylvester, Kevin
        Game day : meet the people who make it happen / Kevin Sylvester.

ISBN 978-1-55451-250-8 (pbk.).—ISBN 978-1-55451-251-5 (bound)

        1. Sports—Vocational guidance—Juvenile literature.
2. Sports—Juvenile literature. I. Title.

GV734.3.S94 2010   j796.023   C2010-903864-9

Distributed in Canada by: Published in the U.S.A. by:
Firefly Books Ltd.   Annick Press (U.S.) Ltd.
66 Leek Crescent   Distributed in the U.S.A. by:
Richmond Hill, ON   Firefly Books (U.S.) Inc.
L4B 1H1   P.O. Box 1338
                                   Ellicott Station
                                   Buffalo, NY 14205

Printed in China.

Visit us at: www.annickpress.com
Visit Kevin Sylvester at: http://kevinarts.blogspot.com

To Doug, Tim, and Mike – three great brothers and teammates.
– K.S.